CONSTRUCTING

your

CAREER

ELINOR MOSHE

Interior design: Ida Jansson

National Library of Australia Catalogue-in-Publication data:
Constructing Your Career/Elinor Moshe
Success/Self-help

ISBN: 978-0-6488839-9-9 (sc)
ISBN: 978-0-6488839-1-3 (e)

This book is dedicated to:

My parents, who constantly provide unconditional support pursuing any achievement.

Ron Malhotra, for giving me what no one else could and what I needed the most.

And to you, dear reader, for seeking to be exceptional and unveiling what is possible.

Contents

INTRODUCTION

Did you know you are the only person with agency and control over your career? Over 90% of your career is determined by your own decisions, thinking and desires.

Did you know with the right mentoring, development and structure, anything is possible? I mean it. There is no ceiling to career, except the one you have built yourself.

Did you know you already have the most important tools in your toolkit to make that happen? It's your ambition and your mind.

What if I were to tell you the conventional career intelligence publicly available surrounding careers in construction has mostly held you back? This is the case for a few reasons. First, it's incomplete and missing context. Second, it doesn't provide a holistic approach to career development. And third, it's missing all the internal work that's first required to achieve career success, because we live from the inside out.

Unlike actual constructing contracting, if you're relying on external parties to yourself to do the construction work for you, you're leaving opportunities on the table. While you'll get the chance to work on some brilliant projects throughout your career, there is only one project which is the greatest. Only one project you will ever get to work on that will yield the greatest results; it's you.

That's why I needed to write this book for you.

Because time and time again I see people working harder (not always smarter) on the projects and forgetting to work on themselves. And don't let tenure or years in industry fool you. Just because someone has been in industry for decades doesn't mean they have ever stopped to consciously consider their career. Whether you are about to embark on your career in construction, or are well into it, this book has something in it that can serve you.

You could spend years accruing bits and pieces of career intelligence for the construction industry, and that's what it has taken me. While you'll never stop developing yourself and inherently your career, I will fast-track the foundational insights you need to build your career in construction. I will unveil insights, advice and practical steps that will allow you to fast-track your career and to propel yourself into achieving more.

Wouldn't you like to achieve more in half the time?

This book will only work for you if you're wired in the following ways:
- You're not afraid to do the work and can demonstrate enough discipline to get results.
- You won't quit when something doesn't work out for you after one trial.
- You're ambitious, driven, and dedicated enough to play the long-term game.

I wrote this book for you from a place to guide, inspire and direct you to achieve more recognition, higher compensation and faster career progression. I will be matter-of-fact with you and tell it to you like it is. I have shared insights I have gathered over the course of my career and insights I have deeply considered to shape my career. I have parted insights with you I had, or I wish I had as I was propelling through my career. That's because I know what it's like to feel lost, stuck, stagnated and wanting to turn to just one resource to tell me what I wanted to know.

Are you ready to come on this journey with me to construct your career? Let's go!

MY JOURNEY

For as long as I can remember, I have been labelled and considered as career-orientated and career-driven. This may have more to do with my focused ability to be extremely dedicated in pursuing goals and achievements which yield results, most of which have fallen in the professional arena. There is one particular moment which continues to stand out in my memory bank. I was in Berlin on the 'Euro Trip' that is accustomed to being had on your gap year. My friends and I were in a dorm room in a hostel and we were playing some game to kill time on a grey, rainy afternoon. (I was twenty-one, the only point in time where I could accept such accommodation.) At the time, I was working part-time in retail and had just graduated from my Bachelor of Environments (Architecture). We were going around the group and everyone had to say a word to describe the person in the hot seat. In full concurrence, without even a round-table discussion, I got "career-driven".

It struck me and perplexed me at the time. First, because I didn't even have a career by a corporate definition then. And I'd 'failed' to get an architecture position during my gap year by successfully not having a folio or performing well by any measure at the two interviews I managed to get. I also just enrolled into my Master of Construction Management, after abandoning the illusion I would be the grandiose architect I once dreamed of, so I was feeling even more uncertain of the future. Let's not forget, I also had no intention of pursuing industry employment until graduation, as I was under the common misconception that a degree was necessary for starting your career in construction. (More on that later.)

Yet, I was the career-driven one. It stayed with me for the duration of the trip in Berlin. Only as my actual career was off to a start, did I comprehend and understand what it means to be driven by your career. What it means is consuming your time with meaningful work. It means relying on your intrinsic motivation to propel you forward, against all odds. It means finding work that is an energetic match to your spirit and soul. And it means putting the development and actualisation of it over and above other pillars of your life, but not via the sacrifice and compromise of other equally important pillars. It's an artform to do that alone! We'll continue to explore the notion of a career as the book progresses. But isn't the notion of a career such a loaded word, full of connotation and alternative world views? Isn't it such a fascinatingly complex concept that few individuals truly spend the time unpacking and understanding? If anything, I have always been conscious of the sheer quantum of hours in our life. This one life we get, that is invested (I say invested in lieu of spent because there are returns on this investment) engaged in career activities, like going to work. I knew from early on it would be irresponsible, negligent and ignorant to not understand the mechanisms, metrics and drivers of my career. Of your career.

While it may be complicated enough navigating a conventional career, I'd the added benefit of getting the filter of construction. I frequently look back on my journey and wonder how, out of all industries, did I end up in the building industry? It was obviously meant to be that way, as the alternative was to become a lawyer or a doctor, like every set of Jewish parents wish for their child to be. How limiting of a framework it is to pick your work based on a job title. It's like saying the job title gives a young individual the full scope of what the career path involves. Far from! Only in retrospect can I connect the dots that lead me to the construction industry. It started in Year 12, where apparently, I then possessed some natural drawing and artistic ability. Now, I wouldn't be so sure. Graphic design was one of my favourite subjects, and for one of the folio requirements I said I would design a building. As I am writing, I am smiling, in memory of how far-fetched the idea was at the time. It was a timber structured restaurant IN the water, with cantilevered glass boxes as dining areas, and the back of the house within the central core. Ten points for creativity, and none for real-world application. However, that wasn't the aim. It was through this folio I discovered I enjoyed thinking of buildings, looking at them, especially in expensive design magazines. It was probably the iconic images of buildings with the architect's name up in lights, photographed like the revered which made me want to pursue architecture. Well, before that, I wanted to do industrial design but was thankfully rejected.

So, on the morning of my 18th birthday, I woke up to my emails in Haifa, Israel. I received the confirmation I was accepted to the Bachelor of Environments (Architecture) undergraduate degree at the University of Melbourne. It felt like an accomplishment within itself, but ignorance is bliss and little did I know what was to ensue. Do you remember how amazing it felt to get that letter of acceptance?

Let's just say while I kept a well above average GPA during my degree, I was anything but a rising architecture star. The design process frustrated me, and I never took joy in it. I was the student who came to class with a "conceptual" model, still with the glue drying and probably dripping. I'm extremely lucky I have an incredible way with words and could spin a skewed story around a skewed model. Trust me, it wasn't without effort or application, but there was little reward for me. I did the all-nighters, the excessive coffee drinking (which is one reason I don't drink coffee today), but it was always driven by a deadline or an assignment, never from a place of love. Plus, the students who seemed to do really well were those who'd the most illogical, impractical designs generated by CAD. I never learned 3D anything, nor had any ambition to do so. With those wild Revit designs that were doing so well, I always wondered how this could ever be built. Who would even pay for it? The floor plates weren't even lining up! And then here I was trying to enter the marketplace with an average folio and no technical skills... In retrospect, I am glad that didn't work out for me.

During the last year which I thought would never come, myself, and a group of friends who maintained the architecture profession, volunteered to organise an architecture exhibition for the faculty, with works from Chilean architects. That was the instigator for helping me realise my personality is far more logical and process orientated. I was more curious to find out how can the end goal be brought to life with all the moving parts. Plus, I'm a chronic planner and highly enjoy organisation, so this exhibition of ours really brought out the junior Project Manager in me!

So, I took the chance, and I enrolled in a Master of Construction Management. It was a complete departure from architecture, having realised I'm not suited to that discipline, and I would like to earn more than the minimum wage. In 2013, I started my Master of Construction Management at the University of Melbourne and it opened my mind to the world of Construction Management. It was everything at once—too big to handle, captivating, logical, structured, overwhelming and answered my questions how we get down to business and make things happen.

Fortunately, I realised conventional thinking wouldn't serve me and I needed to attain employment before graduating. Unlike my time during my bachelor's degree, I was engaged in the classes and coursework of my Master of Construction Management degree. I applied myself, took it seriously, and spoke up in class. You'll see why this matters in a moment. It was first week, first semester I realised quickly I knew no one and nothing about this industry which caught me out during my undergraduate, so I made conscious efforts to network. (More on that later.)

It was first year, second semester that I partnered with someone else in class for a presentation. It happened we were standing outside in a group and I asked the person next to me if she wanted to work together. She was working for a small builder-developer at the time, who were hiring. I rejected the first offer to go in for an interview as I was going overseas at the end of the year. A few weeks later she told me to just go in for a chat, so I did, and was offered a position. I vividly remember being up in the law library of the University of Melbourne when I got the call I was being offered a salary-position. My career was starting. Do you remember the weight lifting off your shoulders when you got your first yes?

I share this journey with you so you can see no matter where your starting point is, you too can achieve greatness in your career.

Circling back to the formative years of my career where I knew nothing about the industry, it took years to piece it all together. To get a visual of the industry on the macro and micro and with all its moving parts and intricacies. I needed to make career decisions based on imperfect information and not knowing any better. Would I have made different decisions? Well, it's always easy to assess in retrospect. But it dawned on me not schools, not universities, and not a handful of networking events could cohesively piece together the industry for those standing at the precipice looking in. It was the original impetus to found my business, The Construction Coach.

There have been many defining moments during my career in construction which have served as valuable lessons and shaped my experience, along with the insight I have developed, to consciously and openly share with my community. Did I ever expect to be authoring a book? During retirement, yes, I figured by then I'd have something to say. It was on the back of a tutoring session with a construction student, which I used to do for two-and-a-half years after graduating, that we were talking about careers in construction. And the student said, "Why don't you write a book?" I laughed, and said, "What would I write about?" It is a commonality you should write a book about whatever it is people always come to you for advice and insight on. Well, I found out early for me that is career advancement in construction.

So, here it is. Constructing Your Career. One of the core ethos I share across my creative ventures is that the greatest project you will ever get to work on is you. As I said in the introduction, people put far more effort into the projects they work on for work, letting the decades slip and time go by. And all without ever working on their career, let alone themselves. But I don't want you to just have a job. I don't want a title to define you, for you are more than your job title. Complacency will kill your career and dreams before anything else, and it is rampant today. Complacency is just another form of laziness, and that will get you nowhere. Over my many interactions with people in industry over the years, this has many shapes and forms. It can look like waiting for the HR department to give you a career plan or waiting for anyone else but yourself to decide what projects you want exposure to and work on. It can look like the only time you check into your career in during performance review time to file another form and get your standard raise. People place extreme expectations on their organisations to develop their own career. The only person in charge of the results, outcomes and trajectory of your career is you. Organisations only facilitate opportunity; it is always up to the individual to understand whether that is alignment with where they want to go. This is the ethos I have always maintained and am always in the drivers' seat of my career.

But what does it take to have an exemplary career in construction? What do you need to be doing to construct your own career? Know this, there is one reliant factor. And that is you. Everything you need to construct your career starts with you. I know from experience when someone is pursuing and building their own dreams, they will happily overwrite yours. The first part of construction is to take back the hard hat from others and put yourself in charge. Just like that.

When you have read this through to the last page, which I hope you will, you will have ignited within you this internal force to take the driver's seat of your career and GO. You will realise it is insufficient to just be a technically apt person on projects because the most important metric of career success in the social age is who you are and who knows you. What you know and who you know have little weight in constructing a career that surpasses the standard of average. In today's social age, it takes extreme and massive action in terms of self-development and actualisation outside of the workplace to truly achieve career success. There may be some elements herein that are obvious and simple to do the aforementioned. Yet just because something is simple to do, it is as easy to not do it.

It's also my duty as an industry leader to show you what is possible. When I was going through university and expanding my networks in the formative days of my career, they presented only a narrow bandwidth of career options; Project Manager, possibly a Construction Manager. The upper echelon positions, albeit a founder of a business or executive management, were seemingly reserved for "someone else" but not me—or so I falsely believed. To realise this is all possible for me took years of mindset conditioning and development. (Which is thoroughly explored on my podcast, Constructing You.) It took time to develop vision and lift the ceiling on what we can achieve, which we will delve into in chapters to come.

Despite my career in construction being closer to a decade, it was only at the halfway mark did I experience this consciousness about my career that I am passing onto you via this book. Only when you look back are you able to perfectly connect the dots and the chain of events that led to one thing, and then another. Some may say that's not a long time to 'figure things out', others may say it's too long. But we're never concerned with what others have to say. I highly subscribe to chairman and CEO of Berkshire Hathaway, Warren Buffett's practice, that the process of making a group decision is looking in the mirror. But again, through my business and other ventures, I am here to propel your career. I am here to be the force you need to propel your career. To move along faster, with more confidence, and certainty clarity. Clarity is power, but why? Because you know where you are going. There will certainly be trials and tribulations, detours and deviations along the way, but we must know the direction.

You may be at the start of your career, picking this up in fervent interest and making conscious decisions and directions about your trajectories. You may be a decade in and realise what you've been doing isn't working for you.

So, let's go. Let's construct your career. This book and teachings within won't be for everyone, nor is that the intention or ambition. But I truly aspire to inspire, guide and direct you, and if this book has served you in such a way, then I am at the least grateful and content. It is worth noting to avoid doubt, the career intelligence in this book is to serve you progressively throughout your career. You may just be starting and not see how this all fits in, but as you progress and evolve, and enter many phases, you will utilise the insights shared with you hereon in. Constructing your career isn't something that happens at one point in time—it will be the greatest and longest project you will ever work on.

I want to see you win and achieve exceptional things. And you will.

HOW TO USE THIS BOOK

It will be tempting to bypass some stages, and only apply sections you deem relevant, or necessary. Each stage and sub-stage hereon in build on one another, just like a fundamental build. This is easy to visualise for a building—but for your career?

Introducing The Construction Careers Paradox™

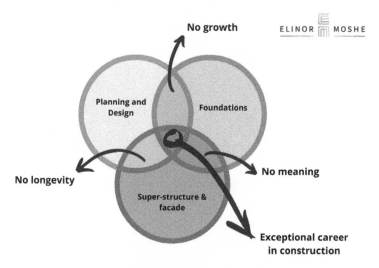

The Construction Careers Paradox ™

If you build your career via planning and design and foundations, there won't be any growth, and growth is essential to avoiding stagnation and fulfilling your ambition and potential. If you build your career via foundations and a super-structure, there is no meaning. A career devoid of passion and purpose, not in alignment with your vision is not worth dedicating your life to. If you build your career via planning and design and with a super-structure, you won't have longevity, or play the long-term game. That's because without solid foundations, everything added to it lacks structural integrity. The sweet spot is in the middle. It's where all the phases and stages of construction come together over time. This is not an overnight solution. You use this book as a guide for the entirety of your exceptional career in construction.

PART ONE

PLANNING PHASE

FEASIBILITY

*"He who has a why to live for
can bear almost any how."*
Friedrich Nietzsche

Is a career in construction for you? Have you fallen into this industry by accident? Have you followed the footsteps of someone who's had an exemplary career in the industry, thinking it can also be for you? Is a career in construction what you want to spend your waking days on? Let's cut to the chase. A career in construction is not sexy. It's not a sexy industry, like wealth management or property. It's a disjunct that can provide friction. On one hand, the advocacy for the industry is high, but on the other, how attractive is it to work in this industry? Whenever I am painting the picture of opportunity in the industry, I also paint the lesser attractive side, with challenges. When I was tutoring after the completion of my master's degree, I'd a student who was starting their diploma and was immensely struggling. Before I started with the session, I would ask students why they wanted to work in construction. This particular student told me he wanted to be a Construction Manager because of the "big dollars". I then broke the news that this is not where you start off in industry. Depending on the sector, it could take anywhere between 10-20 years, and there were many factors that would contribute to that happening. The enthusiasm faded quickly, and I saw his gradual disinterest in the content. He sent me a message the next day saying he dropped out of the course because in all actuality, he didn't really want to do construction. That is a fantastic outcome because it saved him years of study and debt doing something he wasn't interested in. You can't force someone to be interested in timber construction. You really can't.

The rewards in the industry far exceed remuneration, which is commonly touted as the selling point. Yes, the salaries are higher, but they also reflect the hours, risk and responsibility taken on. For some, having a career in construction is about legacy whether that be working for a head contractor, quantity surveyor, subcontractor, and all the inherent positions, from Project, Site, right through to Construction Manager (to name a few). It's the chance to contribute to cities and social fabrics and leave something behind that might withstand the test of time. It's the chance to create one of humanity's most basic requirements—shelter, right through to creating monuments that generate awe and inspiration. It's the chance to craft what was once thought impossible until it was done. For others, it's the satisfaction of taking a step back at the end of the day and seeing what they worked on, right in front of them. Construction inherently is a creative process. While it looks systematic, and is, it's creating something where there was once nothing (or something else, which is what refurbishments are for).

The construction industry offers immense intellectual challenges that brings in construction, technology, architecture, business, legalities, and even ethics, all together, from a management perspective. Plus, the opportunity for those who love to get their hands dirty and produce something tangible is also there. Working in the construction industry also has a unique way of shaping your capability. Take your project management ability as a whole—you can easily initiate, plan, execute monitor and control projects for yourself. I was talking to an industry colleague who runs a services consultancy firm and was not phased at all about his upcoming build for his house, that he was project managing himself from the ground up. It's not the technical ability, it's having developed frameworks in place that render you capable to apply yourself to any project. Because of the fast-paced dynamic environments, your ability to make fast-decisions is developed. Who you can become and develop into because of working in the construction industry offers a world of opportunity, possibility and chances.

On the other hand, it's a highly conservative industry known for its long hours, high levels of burn outs, highly competitive (on an individual and business level). The industry is also inflicted with its high-risk environments, mental health issues, unconscious biases, sensitive to booms and busts, to name a few characteristics. There are many misconceptions, such as the only way to succeed is to "pull long hours". And yes, if you are site-based, you must drive to wherever that site is, which is not always close to home. The construction industry is above all a people industry, so if you fundamentally dislike people, then I would also recommend rethinking your career. The industry is rightfully conservative and slow to adapt, because margins are generally low, and problems can cost a lot of money. As I said, it is a people industry, and sometimes you can deal with horrible ones (like any industry).

From the outset of your career, you need to decide: are you merely interested in a career in construction, or are you committed? If you're interested, it's the equivalent of window shopping, or telling the shop assistant you'll think about it when you really won't. Interested won't get you career progression, achievement, and place you above the competition. What you need to be is committed. Committed to your career in construction, because this is the level of dedication, perseverance and resolution needed to be in it for the long-haul. I only know how to play the long-term game. The only shortcut I can give you is to play the long-term game, and this requires unwavering commitment. This is part of ascertaining the feasibility of a career in construction for you. Is it a go, or no go? You should check into your level of commitment frequently because it is what will orientate you to not just doing the minimum but doing what it takes to have an exceptional career in construction. Why do you want to enter one of the most difficult, demanding and stressful industries?

A career in construction on the whole requires you to play the long-term game because there are many elements to master which take time. For example, learning how to build if you wish to have a path on the project delivery side can take multiple project cycles to not just understand it for yourself, but to explain it to others. You both have the technical side to develop, as you do people mastery. Your career is like running a business, which is the approach you need to take. Or I should say that it's like running a project. It takes time to get it off the ground, and strong foundations are imperative to having a viable career. The pay and remuneration definitely come but I see it often that graduates want to transfer in from non-cognate industries because of the possible lucrative pay. You'll get the attractive salary because it is a marketplace that pays above average as it is. But if money is your only motivator, you won't last in the industry. When you're potentially on site at 9pm after a 6am start, money won't be what's keeping you there.

It is worth reviewing the feasibility of higher education in construction. It is well recognised that a degree is not a requirement to start your career in construction. What you need is for someone to first give you a chance. Larger organisations may have this as a minimum requirement to apply, but if you've entered the industry without one and have a successful track record of delivery, it's not a weighted requirement as much. Traditional academic learning is rather antiquated and relies heavily on rote learning. Whereas construction is dynamic, fast-paced and based in the practical and rather than the theoretical. There's a saying that once a graduate enters industry, they go through a period of 'un-learning'. It's just that building construction and the practicalities cannot be fully taught in a lecture theatre. However, attaining a degree generates other attributes and benefits, such as a network and ability to commit to something and hopefully follow through with it. Choosing to pursue higher education is a personal choice and not a mandatory requirement. There are ways to bypass the system and above all save the time required to get your foot through the door. Degree or not, you must get into industry as soon as practically possible, because the degrees are too long. You don't need to wait for graduation to commence the job hunt. The other issue is that today, degrees are cheap in value because they are so common. University certainly doesn't prime you for the world of employment—not in a professional practice sense and not in a comprehensive way to attain employment. I see it happen all the time. Graduates entering the market basing their value on a degree, but so is everyone else, so that is no way to stand out. What matters the most is your set of attributes, cultural alignment to an organisation and willingness to learn. At entry-level positions, companies aren't looking at your great technical aptitude. That they can teach. They're looking for the unteachable, such as drive, ambition, hunger, passion which is why your 'why' matters.

Just because you have a degree in one discipline doesn't mean you are bound to working in that industry forever. This is an absolute career myth. A degree doesn't dictate your future, nor does it limit the options. If it was, I would have been trudging through a miserable career in architecture. There may be some skills bridging required, but that is easily achieved. I am talking in the context of the built environment and not going from construction to medicine. Just because you paid for the degree and did the time doesn't mean you are bound for a lifetime of professional dissatisfaction to see it through. A close inspection will reveal that many careers have far deviated from the title of their degree, and if that's what you need to do, you do it.

As with any business venture or new project, it is imperative to know why. What's the 'why' for starting this business? Why is this project important? Why is this the best idea, the best venture, the best way to go about it? For you, it will be why do I want to develop and succeed my career in construction? What does it mean to me? Why am I doing this? Maybe there was something in your past which has pushed you here and sparked that interest. Maybe you also have romantic notions about reshaping our cities. Because there are many benefits to working in the construction industry, which I want you to harvest and reap and achieve. It will also come with unique challenges and pressures which you will overcome with perseverance, strength and resilience when you know *why* you are doing something. When you set out on a journey, are you willing to accept it when the going gets rough? Or do you only want to go on it if it's all good? If it is for the money, you will burn out quickly, fail to have a holistic approach to career and life, and above all, wake up every morning in potential dread about going to work. Not to say that every day will get you bouncing out of bed—we all have our moments. But, on the whole, when you can articulate and convey your why, those days will get a lot easier. This isn't just an exercise for those starting out. I've had many conversations with people well into their career and can only come up with a basic "because I enjoy it". I also enjoy yoga, but you don't see me making a career out of that. Go deep on your thinking 'why' and don't come up with a sexy reason just because it sounds right. Tap into the curiosity that attracted you to the industry in the first place. What you will find is the best answers are inside of you, and internal alignment with your why is always more powerful than external reasoning.

Career Success

"You don't have to be a genius or a visionary or even a college graduate to be successful. You just need a framework and a dream."
Michael Dell

Part of a feasibility study is identifying the markers of success. You would only pursue a certain development if the numbers stacked up, but that is a literal example. For career application, it is while undertaking a feasibility study, from the outset, you know the markers of success. You know the return on investment; you know what you'll get out of it. Most people never spend the time to generate markers of success for their own career. Maybe one day you'll become a Managing Director, but does that mean success when you know you have more potential? Perhaps you have "climbed the corporate ladder", but does that mean anything to you? Perhaps you've started your own business turning over $10M of projects, and that's a success because you've built the life and lifestyle you desire. Failing to know what success means to not just your career, but your life, is empirically important. As Anne Sweeney, formerly the co-chair of Disney Media confirms, "Define success on your own terms, achieve it by your own rules, and build a life you're proud to live." Otherwise it's like navigating a path without a compass. How do you know where you are going? When I first started my career, I'd a linear focus on "getting to the top". I'd no idea what that meant, where the top was, and what I'd to do to get there.

As the years went on, and I grew as an individual, I realised there were other pillars in my life equally as important to me that surpassed job titles and moving into the next pay bracket. While I achieved the titles and the pay early on, that wasn't feeling like enough, which is what instigated me to realise, I need to define what success means to me. What success means to me, on my own terms, and again, devoid of any externalities. The definition didn't come overnight; it took months of refining. You will also see success isn't a destination; it's a constant state of being. And your happiness is not tied to achieving success. It's not a "if I am successful, then I will be happy." It has nothing to do with material objects collected because of being successful. Financing a sports car you can't afford if you lost your job doesn't equate to success. Yet people see the sports car and think that person must be successful. Realise they could be horrible at their job and make poor financial life decisions. Success comes from within. And that definition will evolve and grow as you do and realise what you are continuously capable of. This definition is devoid of any job titles, pay brackets, years of experience. It is a holistic view encompassing all pillars of your life that will serve as your compass. But there is one extremely important factor in your definition which must be included: who you are.

There are four metrics of career success in the modern day: what you do, who you know, who knows you, and who you are. Two of these have more weight than the others. What do you think they are? They're who knows you, and who you are. Conventionally in the construction industry, we place the most weight on what you do, which reflects your technical capacity. In my opinion, your technical aptitude only accounts for 10% of your career success because we can teach technicality to anyone who has an ability to comprehend (whether they are interested is a different story). Where people falter as they move up the chain, is they continue to solely rely on their technical skills to attain progression, higher remuneration and recognition. They place all their efforts during the workday to get technically fantastic. But technicality doesn't make you a great manager and has nothing to do with leadership. If your sole value proposition is technical aptitude, and what you do, then you are replaceable. Who you know is also commonly touted as a metric. It is important to have a broad network in the industry, but you may know 100 people, but only two people know you. You may claim to know person X, but will they pick up your call? This is why who knows you and who you are, are the most important. Those who know you show you project influence, and when you are in any position, you will need people to come with you. Maybe it's a decision you need them to agree on. This also serves to demonstrate your leadership capacity, because you can tie in your why with the why of others, and that's how you get them to come with you. But the ultimate factor that will determine your career success is who you are.

*"If you don't know who you truly are,
you'll never know what you really want."*
Roy T. Bennett

Who you are speaks to your character and personality. Do you think you can be the best Project Manager you can be if your character reflects accepting poor standards, lacking integrity and high morals? I have seen it and heard of it time and time again. Project managers, who are technically fantastic, but get subcontractors to do a bit of work on the side for them and charge it to the project or promise them a win on the next tender. You want to tell me that is success, or the marker of an ethical individual? No, it's taking advantage of the system which has served you well. What's worse is upper management tolerates this performance. In that example, *who* that person is, is a below average person. People are connected to other people, and more deeply so when they perceive authenticity and consistency in the person. People are drawn to aspects of your personality. The more you know your authentic nature, the more you can project that, and the more you will find you'll attain coveted leadership positions and also success beyond a technical capacity, at minimum.

The issue with this is understanding who you are in the absolute macro and micro is work. It takes a hefty investment or time and also finding the processes which allow you to do that. It's both an art and a science. In today's social age, it takes extreme and massive action in terms of self-development and actualisation outside of the workplace to truly achieve career success. A one- or two-day professional development course on a generic skill has negligible impact on accelerating and building a career. What matters most today is who you are. Your personality, your values, your attributes. If you don't spend the time to figure this out, you will spend decades free-falling into positions and working much harder than you should be. Why would you even dare to leave this to chance? You can start by making a list of things you always do, or things people say about you. For example, I am confident. I know it, it's in my nature, and I naturally exert it. Yet overtime I dulled that down because it made other people feel uncomfortable, and as a result I wasn't being who I am. I was being what I thought others thought I should be, which is all wrong. Once I shook that off, by doing the work, I embraced my confidence and own it to its fullest extent, and how I show up to every scenario.

But who you are now may be an underdeveloped version of who you need to be, to achieve the level of success you want. This is one of the core reasons I based my podcast around the becoming part of your career development. First, you need to become, and then you achieve. I share the stories of the people behind the projects on my podcast, to show you who you can be. To show who you need to be, and need to grow into, to achieve massive career success like the guests on the show. Regardless of your job title, regardless of where you have come from or where you are right now. I said before that 10% lies in technicality. Well, the other 90% lies in your sphere of impact and influence, which is only possible when you first work on yourself. You don't get to have massive success without first growing into the person who can achieve these big goals. Because what is the greatest project you'll ever get to work on? It's you. It's the person you have to become. The people who have founded companies that turn over millions—they were first, decisive, direct and risk takers. The people who are Managing Directors, they're not meek, indecisive and lack confidence. It's the opposite. The people who are exceptional Project Managers—first, they become great leaders, build exceptional delivery teams, then they achieve the recognition of excellence in project management. In your definition of success, it's extremely important you determine the person you want to become. Otherwise you will lose yourself in building a career and find one day you have no idea who you are because that's attached to your job title and what others have expected of you.

It was touched on before, but success has to look holistic. Would you claim someone a success if they'd all the professional accolades and delivered the greatest projects, but had serious health issues and zero spirituality? I certainly wouldn't. This is never something people tell you when they're talking to you about your career, but by reading this book, you're bypassing years of not knowing this. I was working on a large, complex project that was a high stress environment because of the project parameters and awfully demanding client. To some extent, rightfully so, they'd extremely tight deadlines and a lot of project stakeholders to please to say the least. When I first started on the project, the Senior Project Manager was as you would call, 'old school'. He'd a particular way of doing things on projects and certain expectations that weren't in alignment with modern management styles. As the project progressed, said manager started dealing with health issues, as long drives teamed with long hours and a highly stressed environment didn't allow for health to become a priority. You have to know that not having time is merely an excuse. It's all a matter of priorities. Those health issues which were overcome, I saw over time, he started realigning his priorities. It was in one conversation where he openly told me health and family would take precedence this year. About time because he said he'd already done the decades of sacrificing—the hours, the years, the missed moments, and now that needed to take priority. He started questioning what it was all for. But now, he wanted to enjoy life, slow it down, do the things he never got to do because of work. By all means, this manager possessed extreme technical aptitude, could make tough decisions and follow through and was generally commended for his performance. From a career standpoint alone, he was a success. I saw him implement his newfound priorities—leaving at 3pm to pick up his granddaughter from school once a week, and that brought him so much happiness. Then, one Friday before a long weekend, he walked out of site as per usual. Except he didn't come back. He passed away a few weeks later from a sudden health complication, and was lost forever to family, friends and the project team. Rest in peace and thank you for everything you ever did for the team.

I'm openly sharing this story with you, so the last day you get to experience on this earth isn't your workplace. Because you'll never know when it's too late to adjust your priorities, and realise what not just a successful career, but a successful life entails. I was hesitant whether I should share this story with you, in the context of a book about constructing your career. But I needed to highlight the point to you of making sure in pursuing success in one arena, you don't attain it at the cost of total negligence in other equally as important arenas, such as health. Be career-driven, be career-focused, but apply that same gusto to other aspects of your life. This is feasible.

BRIEF

"If you don't make the time to work on creating the life you want, you're eventually going to be forced to spend a LOT of time dealing with a life you don't want."
Kevin Ngo

Practically speaking, the purpose of a project brief is to define and capture the core objectives of the project, the scope of works including key deliverables, and the budget and schedule. This consolidated document allows all relevant stakeholders to have one focused and desired outcome that the collective can achieve.

So, now you can tell me, what do you want?

Can you tell me what you want in vivid detail, perfectly scoped, specifically?

What do you want from your career in construction? You know why you're pursuing one, and what a successful one at that looks like, but what do you want? I couldn't answer this question for years.

A previous mentor of mine would ask me consistently, and I would constantly draw blanks. Once I conjured up the answer I wanted to work on site, which I was already doing, but that was as far as I could extend myself. Alternatively, I would churn out job titles, which is not a weighted response because that is not the extent of your potential. At other times, as I mentioned it to you before, I would confidently say I would get to the top. But I couldn't tell you why that was the case, or what it would mean to me, and my family and community once I got there. To throw it into the mix, I would say I wanted to be successful without knowing what that looked like. All the insights and advice I part with you in this book, I have experienced, applied and grown from. I could never ask someone to do something I won't or haven't done myself; that is not a high standard. But for the first few years in the construction industry, I really struggled to articulate what it is I wanted. That's because first, I couldn't see what was possible for me, and second, I hadn't spent more than several minutes sitting down to figure this all out.

It's my duty as an industry leader to show you what is possible. When I was going through university and expanding my networks in the formative days of my career, they only presented a narrow bandwidth of career options; Project Manager, possibly a Construction Manager. As I mentioned before, the upper echelon positions, albeit a founder of a business or executive management were seemingly reserved for "someone else" but not me. To realise that this is all possible for me, took years of mindset conditioning and development. It took time to develop vision and lift the ceiling on what we can achieve. Let's bypass the years: anything is possible. There are no positions, opportunities, companies out of limits to you. And you have every capability and capacity available to you to create opportunities the market doesn't present you. Other people will be quick to tell you what isn't possible, because they themselves haven't either tried or are definitely operating out of a narrow world view. But someone who is achieving more than you will never tell you what isn't possible. Only people achieving less than you will place limitations. If you have an itch to start a business, start a business. If you have an itch to specialise in a particular field, specialise. Call it blue sky thinking—when you are sitting there generating your brief, it's blue skies; no clouds, no limits.

To some, this clarity and precision will come earlier than for others, and this is a consequence of knowing who they are, and undertaking that internal development and assessment required. But fundamentally, at whatever stage you are at, know he is the only person in charge of the results, outcomes and trajectory of your career is you. Organisations only facilitate opportunity; it is always up to the individual to understand whether that is in alignment with where they want to go. This is the ethos I have always maintained and am always in the drivers' seat of my career. As are you. The brief is a blank piece of paper where you get to determine in its full glory, what it is you want out of your career. Is it exceptional pay? Challenging work? Flexibility and diversity in the nature of your work? International work? Contech giant? To be the number one consultant and only consultant available who can assess extremely complex delays? Whatever it is, start determining the deliverables.

The brief will be a live document and one that evolves as do you. But this will become important in vetting opportunities as you progress. It will also help with possibility overwhelm. There are many avenues that can be explored in your construction career, and when you're standing at the outset, or even mid-point, well, at any point, it can be overwhelming. When I first realised this, I questioned if I was on the right path for me, and then I fretted about how I would achieve it all. And then good old fear (that wasn't tamed back then) kicked in and had its negative discourse with me. Let's put all that into perspective. Realise that your career will be another 40-50 years. That doesn't mean working your whole life, nor does it mean working until retirement. It's an indication of the decades available to you to engage in meaningful work. Meaningful work does not have to happen solely between 9-5. You can and will have many parallel ventures alongside your main source of income. As you should, because your potential is infinite, and what a waste it would be if that only eventuated in a mediocre job you didn't love. People underestimate what they can do in ten years, but overestimate what they can do in one. The industry titans and exemplary leaders I interview on my podcast have been at it for at least over a decade, if I'm not mistaken the average is certainly over fifteen years. So, maintain the drive and impetus to want to achieve exceptional things in your career but know it won't eventuate in one year. Maybe not even three, but you'd be amazed what can result in ten years. But when you know not only are you in total control of your own career, can do anything you want with it, and you have the time, the overwhelm reduces. It dissipates. Cut out indecision, procrastination and listening to what other people think, and then there will be no overwhelm, just decisive action.

You would have heard the saying that clarity is power, but what does it mean? It is extremely powerful for the mind when you are clear on what you want. People are far clearer on what they don't want, and when you focus on that again and again and attach your emotional state to it, that is exactly what you'll get. Because your subconscious mind can't tell the difference between positive and negative wants. It just gives you what you are focusing on. When you constantly tell your mind what you want, your subconscious mind has a clear objective and direction. With enough repetition, time and belief in the clarity of what you want, you'll start seeing opportunities where there were none before. People and projects will start aligning to you. Things will start happening for you. This isn't a book solely on the power of your mind, but to tap into its power, it truly starts with clarity over what you want. It can also work in that you need to consider what you don't want purely as a process of elimination to get to what you do, but that's what you focus on.

Knowing what it is you want is intrinsically tied to your passion and purpose. They are words commonly thrown around, but without insight into how to discover this, or at a minimum, know you are aligned with this. My basic measure of knowing if I am aligned with my higher purpose is to watch my energy. When I am doing something that is aligned with my passion and purpose, I have immense energy; I go on a natural high. It's the energy I have at my workshops and events, it's how I feel when recording a podcast, it's how I feel when I am in a mentoring conversation with a client. And it's also how I feel when writing this book. In all the above, time just melts away, hours can go by and I haven't noticed it at the least and my energy is still high. Sometimes I don't even eat, I'm just plugging away in a constant state of flow, and then I look up and realise how many hours have passed. That's one way of knowing you are in alignment with your passion and purpose, and that you are working from your zone of genius. Anything else that depletes your energy and leaves you drained to do anything else, is not in alignment with your passion and purpose. It means you are operating on a really low frequency and it's draining you. If that's how you feel on the daily, it's time to realign. This doesn't mean you are a buzzing ball of energy at all times, which is exhausting within itself. But your overall state of being is energised, not depleted. This is one of the easiest ways to understand if you are in alignment with your passion.

There are many schools of thoughts on passion and purpose, and whether there is one overarching reason. I believe we are all uniquely put on this earth for a reason and it is our duty to discover what that is, so we can share our value with the world. I think there is one ultimate reason which we are all here for, and that is to be of our greatest value to serve others. Your overarching passion is a singular reason but will translate into many facets over your lifetime of meaningful work. The beauty is in the journey of discovery and constantly seeing how far you can push yourself and what you can do. It is common for people to want to put people into boxes and singular labels because it helps them understand what it is you do. I can't be put into a box; I am many things and will continue to be so. It frustrates people when they can't come up with a label. I'm a public speaker, podcast host, leader, mentor, business owner, and the list goes on. And you shouldn't feel the pressure to do so either. You can have your full-time employment, volunteer, have a side hustle, start a creative project. It's important when you have an idea that you explore it because all the experiences you generate for yourself lead you closer to discovering your purpose and passion. It's easier to connect the dots looking back and realising everything you did led you to where you are today. You'll find it's harder to connect the dots looking forward. It's important to be led by curiosity and excitement in your career.

Discovering purpose and passion can also be as simple as seeing what you really enjoy doing now. It's a fallacy to say you can't monetise your passion. People have made passions out to be hobbies and not your main source of income. If you choose it to be so, it can be. It is when you operate out of your place of purpose you attract the highest remuneration. The only people who say your passion cannot be monetised are those who haven't done so themselves. Today, with an internet connection, people can commercialise just about anything.

I am all for multi-passionate people who have many streams of interests they want to explore, but you'll see commonalities in this which still results in an overarching passion. Have a day job, and fuel other creative passions outside of that. The thing with passion is while you need to think about it, you also need to monitor your feelings. Passion comes from the heart. And the only way you can monitor that is by doing. Take action on your ideas and experiences as they come about, rather than sitting on the sidelines speculating if this is or isn't for you. Get in there and try your absolute best. That's how you'll know. If that means transitioning sectors within the industry, you do it. If it means starting your own business, you do it. And if it means volunteering, you do it.

Another way of uncovering your passion and purpose is to pay close attention to what people come to you for advice on. From the near immediate start of my career, it was for mentoring on careers in construction. This was even before I had visibility, but at events and talks, I would always be approached for career-related questions. That evolved to incorporate many other facets, but it has always centred on the personal and professional development sphere. I don't get approached for advanced construction techniques, or the latest in technology. But watch your energy when you respond. Do you get really excited talking about a certain topic, and you could talk about it for hours on end? With this new mindset, you probably don't even have to go seeking long and hard about what your passion is. It's probably staring you in the face, but fear has overridden your ability to follow it.

Even after reading all this, you may still be conflicted and say you don't have a passion. In that case, I want you to pursue anything you are doing or choose to do with passion. Give it your absolute best, do it with zest and fervour. Call it reverse-engineering the process. Either way, it is a process within itself that requires time and consciousness, and no pressure from within. There is no need to feel like you haven't made it or won't if it hasn't unravelled yet. The more you pay attention to it, the more it will become clearer to you.

Dream big

"Don't let others tell you what you can't do. Don't let the limitations of others limit your vision. If you can remove your self-doubt and believe in yourself, you can achieve what you never thought possible."
Roy. T Bennett

I give you the permission to dream big. When I first started desiring more than what I was aspiring to in my career (remember, it took time to see what is possible). I felt guilty. I wouldn't even vocalise it aloud in fear it would be ridiculed or mocked. I also started questioning my ability to pursue more. But my vision was adamant, and strong, and it was through my journaling practice I let it out. Journaling is my most important creative and expressive outlet. I rarely let a day go by when I don't journal. Journaling gave me the space to dream. To realise even by forming the words on the page meant they were already part of my physical reality and could happen. There is huge power in writing things down, which I will explore in further chapters. I'd done the work via many avenues to see what is possible, and then I took that all in and applied it to my own thinking. I would write pages and pages of many careers I desire, different levels of achievement, and of course, who I can be. It was all-encompassing and required a lot of introspection. Looking inside of yourself for answers the first time around can be confronting and can shake up your reality, which is what it does. I recommend that until you become resolute about your dreams, don't share it with people. Because they will quickly discount them and tell you what isn't possible; this is what happened to me.

At events or in conversation with people in the industry, I've found when I ask them this question, they lean in and speak quietly and in total reservation about their dreams. Or, they will share it but with a disclosure, such as "I'm not really sure". In working up to your big dreams, unhook yourself from the criticism and praise of others. No one has the right to ever mock or criticise your aspirations, but they can always push you to make them bigger. I am a maximalist, not a minimalist, and have no qualms about being in the constant pursuit of more. Society will constantly remind you to play small and just do one thing. That's the first thing that has to stop if you truly want to dream big. Have the audacity to dream, to dream up a career and a life that is truly to your desires. When you realise what that could look like, you never run out of motivation in pursuit of making it a reality. When you sit down to do this exercise, it will become your pull motivation. Having vision is one of the strongest types of pull motivation you can have. And when you give clarity to your vision by realising your big dreams, it becomes easy to dictate what it is you want from your career and life.

"If your dream is a big dream, and if you want your life to work on the high level that you say you do, there's no way around doing the work it takes to get you there."
Joyce Chapman

CONSULTANTS

"Alone we can do so little; together we can do so much"
Helen Keller

It's nice to think we can go about it alone. Perhaps that is a possibility, but it will take an extremely elongated period to achieve the end goal. You don't need to look far for an example. Any construction project, whether we are talking about the physical build and on-site activity, or, the design development that happens in an office, it doesn't happen in isolation. Thinking you can go about it alone and still figure it all out in the least amount of time possible is a fallacy and you're only fooling yourself. The process of leaning into the insight and experience of others is to fast-track your own development. I could spend ten years trying to figure out a process. Or I could access the people who have the knowledge I need to get me to achieve what I need to in half the time. What is remarkable however, is that on an individual level, those who aren't taking agency over their career are the ones who are least likely to invest in assistance. Or do what I call, 'the work' required to achieve anything in it. Yet those who are invested will continue to do so to get the desired results. First, is the latter have exercised the muscle of investing in themselves and their career, and once you see results, especially in terms of accelerating, they keep on doing so. Whereas the latter remain locked in a state of fear and don't have enough foresight to see the benefit. You may also have to accept that while you are at the helm of your career, at times you may be underdeveloped to lead it. Think of a novice entering a Fortune 500 company. Which is why you need to bring in the advice and insight from others. And never be daft or fooled into thinking everything you know right now is all you'll ever need to know. Absolutely not. I mentioned previously your career is like a business and needs to be treated as such. And businesses frequently bring on consultants. You don't want to see the business owner doing their taxes.

The consultants will come in many shapes and forms, and there will be many people along the way who feel like they have the right to impart advice. But it is always up to you whether you will take it. Consultants in this chapter is my reference to two types of 'consultancy'; mentoring and networking. I built my career from networking and mentoring. Other than my person (who I am), mentoring and networking are two fundamental building blocks that has propelled my career and will propel yours too.

Mentoring

"Our chief want in life is somebody who will make
us do what we can."
Ralph Waldo Emerson

You will find as you traverse your career, many people will pre-qualify themselves to be a mentor, generally, and then further so, your mentor. Being considered a mentor is a privilege, and a position that, once bestowed, cannot be taken lightly. I have always seen myself as the CEO of my career, at the helm of the board. And there are a few select seats available which you can fill as mentors (board members) who you can turn to for advice based on their area of expertise. These mentors do not have to be all career related. They will vary in their expertise and breadth of professionalism. I hope you strike gold and find the one mentor who will forever change your life, as that person came into my life and my career and I've experienced nothing but massive transformation and growth. It's a big part of why I'm writing this book for you. As leadership authority John C. Maxwell said, "One of the greatest values of mentors is the ability to see ahead what others cannot see and to help them navigate a course to their destination." But these mentors and advisors are never to override you, overthrow you, or overpower you. Remember, you're always at the helm, and you must never relinquish your agency or power over your career because of someone else's world view.

This leads me onto the considerations which you need to be aware of when entering mentoring relationships. This is relevant to both mentoring that is free and paid services. At the start of my career, I didn't have the evaluation criteria and parameters I do now when choosing mentors. However, first things first, I will only absorb advice or their consideration if I would switch places with them. If I wouldn't, then why would I need their advice? The advice and insight you are seeking should help you get to where you want to go. And if you don't want to go where they are or have been, then question if their advice is relevant to you. If I don't desire the life and results a mentor can provide, then they have no right serving on my board of mentors. That's why you have to carefully assess:

- What results has this mentor achieved in their own life?
- What expansion and transformation can we achieve via interacting/engaging with them?
- Will they bring out the best that is already within you, rather than what they think is best? And,
- Will engaging with them save you time as to where you'd like to go?

It is also critical you look at the career and life your prospective mentor has because that will give you insight as to the weight of their advice. You will find over the course of your life people have limited and narrow world views. A high percentage of the population hasn't reached consciousness and is operating out of a state of sleepwalking through life. So, it is likely they will only pass down advice, (I don't even bring the word insight into the sentence), they have heard, without filtering the context and application. And then if you apply it, you'll just get the same results they have. Would you take financial advice from someone who is severely indebted and on the brink of bankruptcy? I doubt it. I'm sure you'd rather advice from Warren Buffett or Richard Branson. Then it amazes me how people take career advice from people who are ill-equipped and positioned to do so. This is a critical approach, but I am also operating at high standards, as should you. It is also relevant to look at their challenges they've had along the way. If they haven't had any, then they haven't done anything, and not once stepped outside their comfort zone. You need your mentors to have overcome challenges because that is how they will help you fast-track the process by sharing with you not just what it was, but also how it was overcome. If they aren't able to overcome challenges then the strength of their character, again, doesn't warrant them the right to mentor.

When I first started my career, I was fortunate to strike up a mentoring relationship with a senior in the company, which continued once we both parted the company. This mentor was imperative to some of my foundational development within the industry, and someone to who I will always be grateful. However, all good mentoring relationships can run their course. You can, and should at times, outgrow a mentor. At the time when this happened to me, I will be honest with you. It hurt and was perplexing because I didn't know what was happening. I was veering off on a path I didn't know I was yet to venture on, but this mentor couldn't lead me on either. I also learned an important lesson at the end of this mentoring relationship, which I owe you to be open about. It was through a myriad of self-development explorations that opened my own vision about what I wanted. Yet this mentor perceived other ambitions for me and tried to overwrite mine by discounting me as a whole. No one ever has the right to overwrite your dreams, goals and aspirations with what they see fit. That's the part that caused me to hurt, because I'd placed a lot of good faith and trust in this mentor that they should always do right by me. But sometimes the right thing to do is to take them off your board of advisors. That's why it is imperative to know what it is you want and where you wish to go. Otherwise you may end up falling to the whims and dreams of others, which is a total waste of your career, especially if you don't believe in their dreams.

There have been similar people who have claimed to want to mentor me, but I found interactions with them a total waste of time. They were more interested in partaking in mentoring as a token gesture, doing it for the sake of doing it but imparting little value. At first, I thought it was a privilege said person was taking a vested interest in my development. They were much more vested within themselves and had nothing to do with me. You need to be vigilant and cut off mentoring relationships that are not serving you, because if you don't, you're wasting precious time, and there is no more finite of a resource than time. You also need to switch the conversation, and not constantly feel like the privilege is all yours at being mentored by someone else. The privilege is equally theirs, that you have let them into constructing one of your most valuable assets. It is beyond imperative you always maintain control of the meeting, discourse and duration with your mentor.

It is always up to you to seek mentoring outside your organisation. I'd like to know how many ultra-successful people there are who relied on quick 'coffee catch-ups' and mentoring purely within a professional organisation to attain their success. Alas, this is the extent the average professional will consider as mentoring. A mentor within an organisation can prove imperative to your scaling, especially if they become your public relations team and your sponsor. However, this can remain on the professional level, and the internal mentor can really only advise you within the parameters of the position. This also creates the trap mentoring remains in the purely technical sphere. If it solely focuses on how you can be better at doing your job, you're not tapping into the full potential and benefits of mentoring. Organisations automatically put people whom you directly report to as your mentors, and conventionally it someone is a few steps ahead of where you'd like to be. This doesn't automatically mean they're equipped to mentor you. It's typical to see a Project Manager and Contract Administrator form a mentoring relationship, but it is far too based in the technical development of your job. In some cases, this works out. In other cases, it's a limited one, because having management in your title does not presume you have any mentoring capacity. So, shake off the sense of compilation you have to be mentored by a direct superior. Reach higher within an organisation if you must be mentored internally, and vet them against the criteria previously discussed.

There is a common misconception that mentoring should be free, and what prevents people from stretching themselves in a figurative sense and seeking mentoring outside the organisation for the reasons stipulated above. A reason I have propelled like I have is because I have actively invested in this myself, for myself. The issue stems further in that people feel a sense of entitlement to the success of others, by wanting to 'pick their brain' or 'get some quick help'. While some consider this important and a genuinely good thing to do, the onus is on you whether it is beneficial to your career. This is where the case for structured mentoring programs that you invest in from your own accord comes into play. Think about how many free resources are available to you out there, right now. For all intents and purposes, you could Google how to start a billion-dollar company. The pathways of billionaires are openly shared, and there is a plethora of articles with their top tips, top insights, top mistakes. Yet how many people then apply all of this, and get the same results? A percent of a percent, if any. What's missing is the actual commitment piece in the form of energy being exchanged. And yes, that is money.

People are wired to be more obsessed with what they may lose, rather than look at what they can gain. People fail to see structured mentoring programs are well-considered solutions to getting you to where you want to go, but faster. Because what they are saving you is time. You can go make the money back, if you had to, but the time you cannot. The value can be anything from a $50 event to a multiple five-figure course. But if you are not willing to invest in your own career development and wait around for your organisation to do that for you, then you can also expect mediocre and average results. When organisations are thriving, when everything is good, there may be a few professional development days thrown into the mix. When organisations are scaling back, what is the first thing that goes out the window? Staff development and growth, because the focus is on making sure the business is around after the bust. So, if you desire exceptional growth, take your own development into your own hands, and continue to invest in yourself. Do not rely on your organisation to do so.

One of the greatest moves I had made in my career and life is work with the best mentor. Simply, the best. Mentoring is getting the chance to stand on the shoulders of giants. I wouldn't be able to tell you to seek mentoring if I didn't engage in it myself. Advice from people who tell you to do something that they have never done themselves should be immediately disqualified. Ron Malhotra is my mentor and is one of the most exceptional people I have ever met, and probably ever will. It would be a book within itself exploring the expansive and transformative experience it is working with him. I wanted to learn what Ron's program offered; I desired the results, and a quick assessment proved that there was no one else more suitable to mentor me than Ron. Of course, at first, there was an apprehension of the unknown, and a bit of fear, but there was no choice but to move past that. I have always known that if I would like to see out my vision; I need to first invest in myself. There was no other way around it.

And this wasn't the first investment of a mentoring nature I have made in myself. I have gone to the conferences, the events, paid for the online courses. I'll never stop funnelling funds into myself via learning from the best. And Ron Malhotra is the greatest. I cannot bear to think what would have happened if I didn't take up the opportunity to be mentored by Ron. I would have wasted years in the unknown, instead of operating with clarity, precision and certainty. Ron has this unique ability to extract your unique blueprint, magnify it, and hand it back to you. He can see you in ways that you can't see yourself. And Ron wants his mentees to win and succeed more than anyone else. It's because of the work I've done with Ron, that you get to benefit from it too. It's a win-win for everyone. And, I do truly love the exploratory process that unveils itself when you get to work so closely and intimately with a mentor. There is no qualm that you cannot bypass the requirement of investing in yourself in such a way. I know that the more of this I do, the more I can serve my community. It's why I can also direct my community to do the same, because I understand and have experienced the expansion, transformation, and power of it myself.

Networking

"The currency of real networking is not greed but generosity."
Keith Ferrazzi

You've heard the saying; "Your network is your net worth." Have you stopped to consider what that means? It means your net worth from a financial standpoint is the average of the five closest people in your network. If the median earnings of your immediate network are $50,000 but you have aspirations to hit a multiple seven-figure net worth, then it's time to upgrade your circle.

Yet networking is more than just building your financial equity. It is about building your relationship equity. Technically, you can take both to the bank. Whether it is to access the hidden job market, collaborations, or insider information, you need a dense network. When I started my career in construction, little did I realise how nearly everyone seemed to know everyone. I was fascinated, and I wanted in on this. Except once upon a time I was the shyest, quietest, most timid person you can throw into a room and there was negative chance of any networking happening. Yet this was just a story and a persona of myself I was selling myself, and I quickly needed to change that. Because I experienced the difficulty of having zero connections in the architecture industry, I wasn't letting that be the case in construction. Before that, I needed to know why I would actively take on networking. First, it was to build a network before I even needed one, and second, it was to feed the natural curiosity I possessed about the construction industry. And the only way I would accelerate my position and knowledge of the industry was to get out there and talk to people.

And that's what I did. I went to event after event, lecture, seminars, workshops, panel discussions. After the first few intimidating moments, I truly enjoyed the experience of connecting with people and seeing them here and there at other events. It was the start of building up 'acquaintances'. What served me well during the start of my career was finding an association that aligned with my values. Then volunteering within to build my own exposure, and also, purpose, for being at an event. It came with a level of credibility at the time of being part of the association and also made it easy to start conversations. Professional associations can offer immense connections, community and opportunities, so I highly recommend maintaining an engagement with ones that align with your values.

I frequently tell people to network, and it is typically met with resistance and apprehension. There are many underlying negative connotations around networking that need to be understood and eliminated. First, you must know networking is a long-term game and rarely does it yield immediate results. The issue is people are so conditioned to seeking immediate and short-term results as a consequence of the society we live in, of immediate gratification. They're not willing to put in the work, which it is, to build your network. Networking is both an offline and online game, and you have to take people you meet from one arena into the other to form valuable connections. But remember, as American author Michele Jennae notes, "Networking is not about just connecting people. It's about connecting people with people, people with ideas, and people with opportunities." There are accelerators to this, such as market positioning and branding, but this is all in the intention of having people experience your person to establish that connection. Going to one or two events and not getting the outcome (possibly a job) you wanted doesn't count as networking effort.

In 2017, I went to circa 29 networking events, a high majority of them building industry events. One reason I could build an industry presence offline first was that I constantly showed up. Even when I didn't feel like it, I went. Having the network and presence established offline made for the transition online easier. Without a long-term approach to building a network, and you are building it for when you need it, you will quickly run out of steam for it.

Making networking all about you is also from where the pressure is derived. Building a network is also about what you can do for others. In 2017, I wasn't looking for another employment opportunity; I wasn't starting up any ventures; I didn't have a direct need, but people in my network did. I could recommend people to companies with ease, connect problems to solutions. When you become the person who can recommend and connect with others, you propel your career. How, you're asking? First, there is a positive perception that comes with people well-connected. It speaks to the person you are. Second, it puts you in a position to add value, and you should always be seeking to maximise your value proposition to the market you're in. And third, there is opportunity for you to benefit from a connection, whether that be in the form of a return favour or another kickback. This is equity building. And we all know how important equity is to fund your next development, your next goal, your next ambition.

It is fascinating how the building industry is hyper-connected, and that is a consequence of projects. On one project alone, you have a set of suppliers, subcontractors, head contractor including the project team, consultants (architects, engineers, and so on). By the end of the project, you've all bonded because of the trials and tribulations the team as a whole experience. Those people then move onto other projects, and then another, and after a not so long time, you've worked with some key companies in your relevant sector in the industry. Which is why, if you take an adversarial, negative, uncollaborative approach on projects, it will be known and will come back to you. Burning bridges in this industry can prove to be a costly mistake. For example, if you're a Project Manager who's adopted the old-school mentality of 'screwing' down the contractor to turn a profit on your project, it will come back to you. Because one day, you'll really need a favour to get yourself across the line—maybe extra workers on site, maybe a variation to go away, and they won't do it for you. Your everyday behaviour and operations are still networking. It never shuts off. And if you are working for a head contractor, remember subcontractors work for a myriad of builders. They're equally important to have in your network. Look after them, and they will look after you.

While there is great importance of networking within your own industry sector, there is equal weight to branch out. At the start of my career, I was fervent in networking solely in construction-only associations. After a while, I got bored with talking about work after work and also about the same issues and considerations. It wasn't just that, but I was not getting the growth and challenging perspectives and views that networking should offer. It felt like starting from scratch, veering into non-cognate industries and disciplines to network, but I am extremely grateful I did. I started again, going to associations that aligned with my values but were nothing to do with construction. I went to business events, start-up events, design lectures. Not only was this interesting, but I learned quickly about other professions, challenges and opportunities I could bring back into construction. And this is what gives you an opportunity to stand out.

When you get into the room, don't aim to be the 'dumbest'

person in the room. Once upon a time, someone must have been that and made it a colloquialism that has surpassed the test of time. If you go into the room not just with that mentality, but also that positioning, what value do you think you'll get and be able to give? Will the smartest person in the room want to engage with you? Will you be able to make the most of the event? No. What this saying is meant to prove is if you are the dumbest in the room you will learn the most. But will you know what questions to ask? Will you know how to strategically align yourself with the right people in the room? Networking is not just buying a ticket to an event that has drinks and food included. It's a game, and you better be willing to play to win. Before going, there is some preparation required. Perhaps it is reading up on the topic at hand, setting up specific goals you want to achieve from attending. Please, do not be the tick-box person who has to collect five business cards to call it a success. It could be getting out of your own head and stop being so anxious about networking. Adopt the confident persona already within you. Your goal is to be the most valuable person in the room.

Once you have mastered the networking game, you want to elevate yourself by going from a guest in the room to becoming a speaker, panellist or emcee of the event. This comes through constantly showing up online and offline and building your network. What this does is highlights you have something to say worthy enough to have others attend to listen to. A huge disclosure has to follow; being a professional or an expert in your line of work does not automatically translate into being a captivating, engaging, and memorable public speaker. Remember in the introduction I told you about becoming more engaged at university? That led to opportunities to be a guest and keynote speaker at university related events, at which there are typical industry professionals. That allowed the opportunities to extend into the professional sphere, which added up to the runway that allowed me to be on the road of mastery of public speaking. But at first, to get the opportunities, you must show up consistently. For me, it was university events and classes which got me on stage, that when tied with a natural ability to publicly speak, created positive feedback and further opportunities. There is a personal advantage to being on stage, but part of its importance for constructing your career is visibility, which will be explored in a further chapter. This is just one of the long-term benefits of networking which I am highlighting to you, as it provides you with an avenue to emerge into a community and create a name for yourself.

> *"Sometimes, idealistic people are put off the whole business of networking as something tainted by flattery and the pursuit of selfish advantage. But virtue in obscurity is rewarded only in Heaven. To succeed in this world, you have to be known to people."*
> **Sonia Sotomayor**

It may be obvious to some and not so much to others, but the network is where the hidden job market lies. I'd go further and say it is where the market of all opportunities lies. It is where the upper echelon positions are chosen, where the deals are made, where the projects are won. To think you can rely solely on your good and hard work to attract opportunities is outdated thinking that will get you nowhere fast. Time and time again I get calls asking if I know a Contract Administrator looking to move. If I know a superstar graduate who's ready to roll. I can and only will recommend people in my network, and it will be the same for others. For someone to take a vote of confidence on you, they have to know you first. If you want that project management role for the next big project, start talking with the submissions team. Build relationships with recruiters long before there is even an opportunity on the market. All my positions have been off-market positions that have been presented my way through networks. I honestly don't know anyone who has successfully applied for a publicly listed position and was successful.

All this sounds great, and is giving you the impetus to network, but there is something holding you back. There always is, and it's probably going by the name of *fear*. You're concerned of networking in case you say the wrong thing, in case you don't do it right, of approaching someone 'incorrectly'. The issue is when people have to all of a sudden become externally facing. They become fearful because they don't know who they are and are highly intertwined with what other people may think or say of them. Once you do the developmental work, step out of your own way and start, you can abdicate this fear. Yes, I have and will come across immensely boring networkers and people who have said all the wrong things, but so what? I don't remember them. I have also incorrectly referenced companies when talking to people, forgotten names, ran out of questions to ask, but so what? Does that mean you are a terrible networker? No, it means you have some work to do offline to get better at it. There are ample how-to's on networking online. If you are focusing on the fearful side of networking, you are focusing on what could go wrong instead of what could go right. And that is not the mindset conducive to outcomes you need to construct your career.

PART TWO

DESIGN PHASE

PRELIMINARY DESIGN

"All labor that uplifts humanity has dignity and importance and should be undertaken with painstaking excellence."
Martin Luther King, Jr.

Now, we will get to work. But what does work mean? We consume most of our waking life with it, but rarely spend the time digesting the concept and understanding what it means for us. I highly recommend you take the time to consider responses to the following questions:

- Why do I need to work?
- What is meaningful work for me?
- What is my understanding of the relationship between work and money?
- How important is growth, success and value-adding in the pursuit of work?
- What work would I do for free?

When I am sitting at the drawing board of any initial idea or professional venture, I ask myself a few fundamental questions to ensure the work is aligned with my vision, passion and purpose. It's the equivalent of sketching up a preliminary design for a project and making sure it aligns with your brief.

The concept of work should deliver results for the following three pillars: financial, personal and societal. The work you engage in should provide you with remuneration that can contribute towards the level of financial freedom, security or independence you desire. Your work should provide a meaningful contribution to the fabric of society (which construction inherently does) and it should fulfil your personal ambitions, dreams and visions. While it is possible your full-time occupation can provide you with this, it doesn't have to. For me, it is insufficient to just occupy myself with a full-time occupation. I have always had many moving parts in addition to it to feel fulfilled. How that has looked like has changed over the years. When I was at university, I needed to volunteer in not-for-profit industry associations to add to the experience. When I graduated, I was actively involved in returning to university and guest lecturing, and then tutoring. That all led to the founding of The Construction Coach, which has added a whole host of 'moving parts' to my life. This brings me extreme fulfillment because of the impact it has on the industry with what I can do with it to add value to the industry and my community. Even if your full-time occupation can meet the requirements of each pillar, you should question to see if there are additional pathways to explore.

Which is why, as part of your preliminary design, I would like you to come up with a career pathway you'll start designing. A preliminary design bridges the gap between the conceptual design (the inner work and brief you have been working on) and detailed design (which is coming up). It involves some key decisions to be made, such as industry sector, project typology, company size. From wherever you are in your career right now, there should be a level of clarity where your next step will be. Wherever you're going, it's important you 'model' that career. Does a building go straight into construction from preliminary design? (I hate to say it, but sometimes yes.) Conventionally, the design is modelled, considered, general arrangement plans drawn up. But the key idea here is that it is modelled to see how it may look before we build it. People will test drive a car before buying one, walk through a house before buying one, but will rarely, if any, put as much diligence into testing out, and modelling a chosen career path.

There are two primary ways in which you can model a career. A try before you buy arrangement. The first, and the simplest way, is to have conversations with a few people who have walked the path you are embarking on. Or where they are currently at in their career. It's as simple as querying how they got to where they are, why they have made the career decisions they have along the way, what does their typical week look like. You can ascertain insight into the work someone does via a simple conversation. Do this with a few people and you will get a clear picture of what your prospective path looks like. The second way to model a career is to experience it. If you are starting out, then it may look like an internship, or work experience. It can also look like a 'side hustle'. A side hustle allows you to explore an idea from conceptualisation to commercialisation (if you want to monetise it). It's the perfect runway into starting a service-based business. You may have an interest in property development and doing it for yourself is a way to experience it. There are many ways of trailing careers before you commit your most precious resource of time to it.

As part of your preliminary design, now is the time to bring your strengths to consciousness. Research studies have shown when your meaningful work is in alignment with your core strengths at work, you will experience an increase in job satisfaction, engagement and meaning in the work. It's a no-brainer, really. Imagine having to go into work every day working in alignment with your weaknesses. It would drain and derail you fast. Yet, you'd be surprised at how many people free-fall through their careers doing exactly this, because they have never bothered to take the time to figure out their strengths. When you work on your strengths, you are working closer to mastery, and for many, achieving mastery is a source of generating meaningful work. The application of strengths you have mastered is extremely rewarding. I know my dominant traits are being the visionary, the leader, the lead communicator and the analytical thinker. These are some of my strengths. For me, working on highly repetitive tasks that don't stimulate me mentally are my weak points, they're not in my zone of genius. In a typical position, there should be 70-80% of work aligned with your strengths, and the balance falling into supplementary work that is part of your role that has to be done. Unless you're running the show, then you get to decide. Everyone has strengths, and a handful of core functions they are uniquely positioned to do better than anyone else. Here are four ways in which you can uncover your strengths:

1. Ask people who have interacted with you in a professional and personal capacity. Ask a large enough sample of people and you will see commonalities in their answers. I went through this exercise and there was one strength that came back with everyone—my confidence. It is important to listen and recognise what others think you are great at.

2. Pay attention to when you are undertaking a task or activity and are in a state of flow. I get this when I am public speaking. I lose track of time and speak from a place deep within that I don't even remember what I say.

3. Reflect on your defining experiences and undertake an in-depth review how you shaped that experience. Were you the person who lead the team? Were you the person who planned everything and loved it?

4. Take stock of what others come to you for assistance and advice on. Is it your emotional intelligence? Your ability to solve any problem in the workplace?

Another exercise you can do to take stock of your experiences is this: get an A4 piece of paper and split it down the middle. One on side, write down all the personal experiences you have gone through. On the other side, write down all the professional experiences you have gone through. Once you have done this, step back and you will see you have mapped out the definitive experiences on your path. Not only should this boost your confidence because you have seen what you have done so far, but study it closely enough and you will find a unique set of experiences and strengths no one else has. You're in a better position to stand out and market yourself when you do this because you can bring to the table a unique strength based on your experiences. Identifying your strengths is imperative as you must play to them throughout your career. Some mentoring I do is to guide and direct graduates how to gainfully attain employment. They always ask me as we discuss interview preparation, how I answer the question of "What are your weaknesses?" My answer: "I don't have weaknesses, only undefined strengths." You could turn a weakness into strength if you had to, but in an interview, you don't show your weak hand.

Setting Out

"Choices are the hinges of destiny."
Edwin Markham

Standing at the outset of the construction industry looking in can be overwhelming, complex and outright confusing. This partly spurred my ambition to found The Construction Coach. I started out as a weekly blog, and that's turned into sold out workshops, events, a podcast, private mentoring service, and so much more in response to what my community needs. I would initially write about my industry insights, lifting the curtain on the industry. There are little local contextual guides to the Australian construction industry. We expect people to make career decisions yet have limited sources of information. This is made even more limited when there is no one yet in your network which you can talk to or trust they will give you a holistic picture. This issue with that is people end up pursuing work in sectors that don't align with what they want. The feedback for blog pieces that offered industry insight was unanimous in thanks for the clarity to move with confidence and reveal the construction industry to the wider audience. For those who are already working in industry and know your sectors and tiers, I give you permission to move on from this part of the book. However, I find it important to still put it into print because it can serve the people who are reading this and are starting out.

Not only is the construction industry separated into sectors: Residential, Non-Residential, and Infrastructure, there are tiers within these sectors which offer different career paths and opportunities. Crash course; we differentiate companies into their tiers by the value of works they can undertake. e.g. your Tier 1 builders (Prebuild, Multiplex) can deliver a $200 million project, for example, and your CPB, Lend Lease and Laing O'Rourke's of the world delivering on billions of dollars of work. Your Tier 2 builders can undertake work anywhere from a few hundred-thousand-dollar fit-out, to a ~$100M project. Within tier 2 there are also tiers— upper and lower, where you have smaller and larger commercial companies. As though it wasn't confusing enough. Your Tier 3 and under are typically in the residential sector, or only undertaking small fit-out or refurb projects and new residential construction, of say a few houses at a time. We also factor in the number of employees. It's feasible to move from commercial construction to residential, but it's not easy moving from residential into commercial as your career progresses. How to transition will be discussed in further chapters.Standing at the outset of the industry, it is commonplace to get swept up to work for the big names, the ones with the cranes in the CBD skyline. That's because this is also what we see when we look at the major construction projects. During a lot of my mentoring with young graduates, once the picture of what it is like working there, they realised it doesn't match with what they want. As with everything in life, it will suit some people and not others. When I was starting out, I'd no ambition to be channelled into a 2-year graduate program, and I was concerned about being a small part of a big thing, which is what it is like working on extremely large projects. This realisation and acceptance allowed me to target companies that were more aligned. The following criteria will help you consider the projects you'd like to work on, which will inform you of the company that can facilitate this. This doesn't strictly apply to head contractors, it applies for consultancies, subcontractors, developers and the like. The following are a few considerations which you can commence considering what project you would like exposure to, and in further chapters we'll explore considerations of choosing a company to work for.

- **Project size** - larger organisations have projects with a larger value. What this means is more people on the project delivery team, which is required because of the sheer size of the workload. This can result in members of the project team being 'pigeon-holed'. This means you only get exposure to certain aspects of project delivery at a time, and you don't have full exposure or visibility to all aspects on a project. For example, you may be doing defects for six months or may be a project coordinator for one trade package (façade, concrete, etc.). On the contrary, when you go down the tiers, you have more exposure and are far more involved in many more aspects of project delivery, because the size of the team has decreased. A $100M project demands more resources than a $10M. You can think of this as either being a big part of a small thing, or a small part of a big thing.
- **Project duration** - larger projects have longer durations, which means you can be on one project for years. For example, you could be on a CBD tower for five years if you're there from start to finish. The other end of the spectrum is fit-out. Fit-out projects are typically short and sharp. I've done a $4M fit-

out in fifteen weeks, for example. If you want more diversity and turnover between projects within an organisation, look at the size and duration. Some have no interest in doing the same thing year in and out on one project and facing the sameness of it all, which is what can spur dissatisfaction without acknowledging why.

- **Project type** - if you have a bit of an architectural flair, then bespoke, unique and one-off projects may be your thing rather than apartments. Apartments carry a lot of repetition; what happens on level 5 is probably the same that's happening on level 9 in an apartment building. Bespoke projects are one-of-kind, like civic buildings, healthcare, educational, that can have unique structures and spaces. If you're into large, big things, maybe industrial type builds is your thing. In it for the glory, maybe a CBD tower if you're fascinated by cranes and super-structures with incredible finishes and incredible contextual challenges of building in a tight urban environment. Want even more complexity? Hospitals and pharmaceuticals. Project typology is personal and what interests and thrills you. Maybe it's repetition, maybe it's diversity.

Now you know what you want, that needs to be matched with a sector and a project typology. Think about the projects you will want to work on and want exposure to, and then find the company that suits. If you are not too sure, you can approach a company that does a variety of projects to help familiarise yourself with different types. By talking to people in industry and getting a gauge what it is like will also help you formalise this. Don't go to a company because of the name or how great you think they are if you have zero interest in the projects. You will move out of there in no time. It's important to note this because you may find yourself having built houses for years when the whole time you had your eyes set on tower construction. The transition, if feasible, will reverse your career.

You should be selective and considerate as to the company you want to build your career with based on your project desires. This can be as simple as not applying for a client-side project management firm when you want to be working on site. Or applying for site-based roles when you want to be working in a head office estimating position or applying to really small companies and having to do everything in a business; whereas you may have no interest in other aspects of a construction business. If you've discovered during this process you want to start your own business one day, find a company that is a start-up and learn everything you can about how it's done. Remember, an organisation only facilitates opportunity; it is up to you if that's in alignment with your career path.

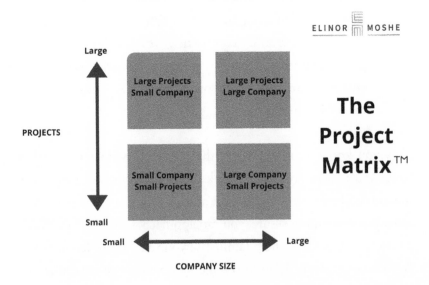

ELINOR MOSHE

The Project Matrix™

The Project Matrix™ shows you the general trade off and relationship between the company size and the project type. Small companies and small projects fall into the tier 3 and tier 4 company. On the complete other end of the matrix you have your tier 1 companies that are large with (very) large projects.

For those who are unsure where to begin, regardless of your desired trajectory, my rule of thumb for those seeking a career in construction is to start off on a site-based role. Or perhaps a position that offers you exposure to a construction site. The first time I went out to site, I didn't have a clue what to do, so I stood there in my hi-vis vest, hard hat and extremely clean steel-capped boots. The site manager asked who I was, and why I was standing there like a bollard. All bright and clean and still. The point of going to site isn't just about being on site, it's about interacting with everyone and the build underway. Understanding simple material technology, processes, how long tasks take and dealing with the people aspect of construction sites to name a few will greatly add to your ability to add value to a project in the future. In all your professional conducts, you must constantly consider how you will add value to the betterment of the project. Because if the project does well, all stakeholders by default do well. I have worked with enough client-side project managers, clients, quantity surveyors who had no real application or understanding of construction. They just had textbook knowledge and poor communication skills which constantly added unnecessary stress and layers of management to a project. Spending one or two years at any stage of your career on actual building construction is not a long time in the grand design of your career. What I loved about the thrill of being on front-end project delivery was the fast-paced nature, and the sense of stepping back at the end of the project and looking at what we've all achieved. I vividly remember my first handover—15/12/15. I'd spent the day chasing approvals and signoffs, and once it was all attained, I just sat there in the summer heat and watched the client move in. I remember thinking, this space didn't exist months ago, and now it will become the place where these people will come every day for important work.

As you are drafting your preliminary design, I would also like you to consider parallel career paths you can develop. They don't all need to start in unison. I discussed before that I always need multiple ventures on the go, it's my natural wiring. But the benefit of that is by having multiple parallel career paths; you can demonstrate your ability to succeed in any application. For example, public speaking for me is not a hobby; I treat it like a career within itself. In everything I do, I intend to be the best at it. Speaking is important to me as it's a chance to create experiences and truly impact my audience. It's a chance to spread a message that will transform my community. Speaking is not just about getting on stage with a microphone. It involves training, practice, mentoring, deep consideration, planning. Excelling in the speaking arena translates into other parallel careers. A parallel career as you work in construction may be property development. It may be leading charitable organisations. Whatever ties in with your passion, treat it like a career and not a hobby, because you will develop skills and capabilities that can cross boundaries of your main career.

Like all designs, they undergo a review. Your preliminary design review should reflect your brief. You should look at it, and go, 'This is what I want my career to start looking like.' This is what a successful career will be filled with and is aligned from everything to your why and your strengths. As simple as this may sound, people go through decades of never figuring this out. One day they find themselves devoid of meaning because they attached their meaning to their job and not the other way around. You have all the opportunity in the world to design your career. There are really no limitations, and if there are limitations that show up, well, our realities reflect our thoughts and feelings. Not doing any of this internal work and design processes leaves people free-falling, going from job to job with no true north. People are far lazier and laxer than you think when it comes to their careers. At some point, I assumed most people were as driven and orientated towards their career as I was and would take full ownership of it, but that is not the case at all. The most common misconception I see is people think their career will successfully unravel before them without any of their input. They believe the organisation will do everything in its power to make sure you succeed in the career of your choosing. I can only encourage and continue to inspire you to see your career as a large, ever-expansive blank canvas in which you get to create the full picture. Only you can see the full picture and determine what you want it to look like. Add as many layers, as many elements as you like, for it is wholly your design.

DETAIL DESIGN

"If people knew how hard I had to work to gain my mastery, it would not seem so wonderful at all."
Michelangelo Buonarroti

The detailed design serves as the basis for the construction phase and is a continuation of the preliminary design phase. As this is an iterative process, you must continue to refine your design to ensure the construction reflects your intention. In this chapter, we will explore considerations needed to add detail to your career to ensure your design can be as complete as possible.

Specialisation or generalisation

At some point in your career, you must decide: specialisation or generalisation. Do you go deep into a level of mastery of one particular aspect, project type, or consultancy? Or do you stay broad, knowing enough about everything that's relevant to your organisation and position? It's the difference between doing one thing really well, and better than everyone else, or doing a lot of things and being good at it. If you're at the preliminary stages of your career in real time, then a detailed design of this may be premature. Especially if you're still trying to find your place in the industry. Or, you may already know your approach. There are benefits and considerations with each.

The rationale behind specialisation is that ability to master and market expertise and unparalleled knowledge in one particular arena is you can demand a higher salary. Think about it in terms of trades. There are some trades who are extremely specialised and are the only ones able to perform an aspect of the works, or they're the only ones licensed in a particular system. They have a monopoly and can charge much more. From this one trade specialising, you can expect high quality outcomes. On the contrary, a trade that performs many functions in different sectors will be cheaper, and the quality will reflect.

Buildings today are far more complex than ever before, with the advent and advancement of materials and technologies that have allowed for complex geometries and advanced performance. With this, there is an immense opportunity to specialise. There is also an opportunity to specialise in project typologies. All of this is, of course, if you want. It is an avenue of opportunity, nonetheless. When you position yourself in the marketplace as someone who has a brilliant track record of delivering a specific project type, you're more attractive to head-hunters and have more ability to influence your salary.

When you achieve mastery and specialisation, you're also in a position to consult back to the industry. You're able to get paid for your results, not just your time. On two projects I worked on, the commissioning was extremely involved as it was pharmaceutical type services. From a risk management perspective, it makes sense to engage the expert on this instead of taking up the time of the general managers on the project who have competing priorities. Commissioning on such projects is extremely detailed, complicated and has to all go as according to plan as possible given it's so close to practical completion. The commissioning consultant could work on his own terms at his own fee, no questions asked.

The trade-off between being a generalist and a specialist is job security. Specialists may be more subject to booms and busts in the industry. To achieve greater reward, there is a level of risk that must be assumed.

If the intention is to specialise within an organisation, the size of an organisation matters. Larger organisations need more people who are specialists, because of the size, scale and complexity of the work they do. For example, they will need a Commercial Manager, whereas smaller organisations either don't need it, or cannot warrant this salaried position. Personnel in larger organisations typically don't wear many hats, they stick to their own lane. Comparatively, smaller organisations will require more generalists—people who can do many things. A project manager may also have to price and win works, and the directors responsible for running the business and bringing in work.

Your focus as your career progresses is to match your ambition as a specialist or generalist. Different organisations will have different demands. Having awareness of this from the start is important as it will also inform you of skills you need to develop. An advanced level of self-awareness is also required to truly identify which category you fall into. Ask yourself:

- Do I lose interest working on the same thing day in day out?

- Would I rather know a bit about everything or a lot about one thing?
- Is diversity in my work and day important, or do I prefer repetition?
- Am I dedicated and interested to mastery of a topic?
- Would I prefer being a small part of a big project, or a big part of a small project?

A combination of both is achievable, and this is by having a diversity of experience that demonstrates both general and specialised capabilities. It's an achievable balance but is a long-term solution. This could be a Project Manager for example who is excellent in civic work but has mastery of programming and delay assessment. The ability to balance and convey this also allows for demand of a higher salary.

There are also major advantages of being a generalist. Workplaces are constantly changing. New solutions and ways of working constantly have to be assessed. A generalist can have knowledge across a broad range of issues and delve into the interconnectedness of it all. A generalist is great at 'big picture thinking' and can see how all the different moving parts come together to create a whole. This can be a Project Manager who has resolute knowledge of all aspects of project delivery but high-level technical ability, thus relying on the specialisation of others at times. A generalist can also be the founder of the business. Founders have a great ability of surrounding themselves with the right people who know what they don't know. It's what also makes them great leaders. It can also be someone who can upskill and learn the intricacies about a new field quickly. Or it could be an Operations Manager who can easily verse themselves in marketing and social media strategies.

What your detail design will be most informed by is the work you've done to date. This will avoid you being swayed by the market conditions and demands. Just because the market may all of a sudden be in high demand for specialists, doesn't mean you need to do so, especially when it's of no interest to you.

Building Services

"Learning to see the structures within which we operate begins a process of freeing ourselves from previously unseen forces and ultimately mastering the ability to work with them and change them."
Peter Senge

You can see the façade, you can see the structure, you can see the beautiful finishes of a building. But what you can't see is the extensive network of building services functioning to keep a building functional, comfortable, efficient and safe. Without an effective services system, all the other aspects of a building are useless. But what does this mean in terms of your detail design and constructing your career? I'm glad you asked.

These are the influences impacting your career that you can't see, and I'll draw some out to bring them to your awareness. This way you can make career decisions knowing what systems are in play.

The first is other people. Other people will be quick to part with an opinion on what your career should look like, what you're suited to, where you should work, and so on. All the inner work you've been doing is to create your own level of resolution and certainty, so you're not swayed or influenced by the experiences and trajectories of others. You're able to forge your own path. Sometimes you can revere someone too greatly that you try to mould your path to suit theirs, but this is going against your purpose and what you're meant to be doing. What others say you can or cannot do is absolutely irrelevant.

"The older you get, the more you understand how your conscience works. The biggest and only critic lives in your perception of people's perception of you rather than people's perception of you."
Criss Jami.

Previous experiences are also influential. You may have had a great experience working on a certain project, with great people who may influence a certain project type or organisation for yourself. Social cognitive career theory details the fact one is more likely to consider pursuing a particular path if they've had a positive experience doing it, because the success is proven, and positive results yielded. What you need to isolate is if this was a consequence because it is in alignment with your brief, or if it was based on externalities. It also works in reverse.

As your career progresses, so does your life. It may be personal, economic or situational circumstances which can influence your career decisions. There may be certain chains of events happening around your career which affects available choices and sometimes even dictating them. In the example of a recession, which the construction industry is sensitive to, always remember that a recession is happening to the economy, it doesn't mean it's happening to you. But in such a situation, it's temporary and may require you to pivot to match the economic circumstances.

PROGRAMMING

"A dream without a plan is just a wish."
Katherine Paterson

You have heard the saying before on an excessive amount of motivational memes. You can have the grandest of designs and largest of aspirations, but without a solid plan to translate that dream into reality, it will always remain just that; a pipeline dream. In my first semester at university, we had to do a programming exercise on a residential property. One reading that came with it was about construction programming and conveyed a simple message. That construction programs were just massive to-do lists. You wouldn't venture out to build a building without a program, yet people do so with their entire life. People spend more time planning their annual holiday than they do their career. Zero plans and lists. It's become so acceptable to just 'go with the flow' and 'see what happens'. That logic will get you into extreme risk and catastrophe on a construction site. It's also the mindset to maintain if you wish to attain zero results, or mediocre and average results. I have rarely, if ever, left anything to chance or at the last minute. I don't even need to look far to see the difference in quality of a career between those who have a plan and direction and those who just let another month go by. Which quickly turns into a year, and then another. As Benjamin Franklin, Founding Father of the United States said, "By failing to prepare, you are preparing to fail." It is as simple as that. It is possible to still have plans but not be rigid and open to opportunities, maintaining agility. There is no issue with pivoting a plan because you have discovered other, faster ways of getting to your desired destination. That is why it's important to have determined your measure of success, because that will act as determining milestones within your program. If achieving financial success is part of your definition, achieving your first six figure salary is a milestone. When you have a plan, you can start breaking that down into goals. How I love goals. I got my first goals diary in 2015 and used the prompts within the diary to write down my goals per category. And to this day, I maintain a goal diary, except now I have an A3 notepad which I write down all my goals because I have that many. Because what I found was when I undertook my reflection at the end of the year, I achieved between 90-100% of the goals written down. Goals written down were achieved, and goals that remained in my mind were delayed, lost and sometimes forgotten. It's not groundbreaking or revelatory that writing down your goals increases your chances of achieving them, because what it does is translate a thought from the metaphysical into the physical reality. The mere fact you've had a thought process, and which has been translated into the form of a goal means it is achievable for you. Writing down goals is how you break down your plan for achieving your vision. Otherwise all people are left with is lofty visions that never eventuate into reality. As with a construction program, it is used to detail what activities happen when. And that is what we must maintain. There will always be distractions and alternative opportunities that will swerve you off program but having a specific plan with goals attached to them helps to prioritise and ensure you are on track to achievement. When you have goals, you have clarity and we know now why that is power. Writing down your goals also tells your subconscious mind what to focus on and the more vivid you detail your goals, the more it is likely to excite you to bring them into fruition. There is ample literature out there on the importance of this, but again, just because something is simple to do, it is simple not to do it too.

Before we get into the tactical side of setting goals, I want to explore some key reasons people don't achieve their goals. There are less than five people who know my goals and what I am working on as it is happening. It is an intrinsic part of my personality that I don't tell people what I am doing, or working on (from a goal perspective, not a workplace perspective). I just show up with the results. I tell people who need to be part of that process to make the goal happen, but that's about it. I'll show you my results and then how I got there. The issue is when people tell other people a goal; it releases endorphins which tricks the brain into thinking you have already done the goal. How often do you get praised when you share a goal? Often, right? Well, receiving a pat on the back for doing nothing will make you less likely, if at all follow through with the goal. You can have ambition, and big goals, but be careful as to whom you share it with. Only share it with people who are action-takers. On the flipside, sharing a goal with the wrong people can attract negative or unwanted feedback, whether it is justified. When you share a goal with the people whose opinion matters the most to you, and they are not onboard, without the mental resilience, you'll be demotivated before you've even begun.

And last, when you vocalise a goal, people can also be quick to tell you the reasons it won't work, why you should try something else. You'll see them apply their own filter and experience over your own, which again, when shared with the wrong person will only hold you back rather than propel you forward. Tell people your goals if you must, but make sure they are more vested in your success than you are.

Not only is doubt entering from many externalities, it is also in abundance internally. How many times have you had a great idea, or detailed an excellent formative goal, but your internal filter of doubt kicked in? It shows up in many forms, such as qualifying you aren't good enough convincing yourself it won't happen anyway. People get discouraged before they've even started. This is overridden by belief. Doubt and belief cannot coexist. If you truly believe in something, there is no room for doubt. Even if you have bouts of doubt, it can't have an emotional connection to it, because those feelings dictate actions. Believe in your goals like they are happening, because they are. They may not happen in the timeframe stipulated, they may not happen as soon as you wanted, but you have to believe they will happen.

It's not enough to be inspired or motivated by your goals, you need to be obsessed. When you are obsessed with your goals, there is no qualm sacrificing. Something has to give when pursuing your goals. Maybe it's the nightly Netflix binge to read a book. Maybe it's giving up seeing friends on the daily to work on you. If your goals can't create that level of obsession, then you haven't dreamed large enough, your vision doesn't excite you enough and you need to go back and dig a lot deeper. For me, to write this book, it was all I did. Day in and out until it was done. Because when you become obsessed, you do the most important thing: taking action on your goals. Most people don't realise their goals because they don't do enough work, or any. When a goal is set, it needs to be broken down into actionable items. It's unlikely to go from running 0km a week to 5km in a week, but it is achievable to going from 0km a week to 500m, then 1km, then 1.5km. But without the work, nothing happens. At least when some work is applied, you can readjust and refine the level of effort required. If you're pursuing employment, for example, making one connection a week isn't enough to access the hidden job market, so you triple it. Imperfect action will always trump no action.

The enemy of goals: excuses, excuses, excuses. It is easy to justify and rationalise why you don't want to do something. Because you've had a long day, because it's not the right time, because you don't feel like it. You need to pursue your goals whether you feel like it, because if you wait for your emotional state to constantly be good, then you won't achieve your goals. Excuses also offer you avenues out, which just fuels further distractions. A goal is a decision. And once the decision is made, it has to be followed through; otherwise you are just exercising average standards of performance. When a decision is made on a project, it is enacted, isn't it? Run your excuses for long enough and you relinquish your level of actionability, and the opportunity to get results. When you don't start seeing results fast enough (because of your goal habits), people tend to quit too soon. It's ok to fail if you have tried your best, but if you haven't tried your best and gave it every single available chance, then that isn't good enough. It isn't an exemplary performance. And how you do one thing, is how you do everything.

To achieve goals, professional or personal, it is first imperative to construct the mindset by which you approach it to get results. It's no different to people going into a project knowing they must achieve certain deliverables and will do whatever it takes. Apply the same mentality you do for achieving your work objectives to your own goals and see how far you will go.

Program

"If you don't design your own life plan, chances are you'll fall into someone else's plan. And guess what they have planned for you? Not much."
Jim Rohn

The program is your plan, and your detailed planning will show the trajectory you have designed with specific information on durations and resources required. My one, two, five and ten years are milestones. At each I know the extent of my grand vision has come into fruition. Then for each year, I write all the goals which I will work on to meet the milestones. If a goal is to be promoted in two years, then you need to work backwards with what you need to be doing today, tomorrow, this month, and next month to make that happen. Without setting a plan into incremental achievements, how will you know if you're on track or otherwise? It's equally as important to set durations. If you want to attain employment, give yourself a six-month deadline. If you leave it open-ended, you will never know if you're doing enough to achieve it. At the same time, assign resources to your goals, which is both time and money. How many hours a week will you spend working towards your goal? And what financial commitment is required? Maybe you need to engage a mentor, buy some more books, attend workshops.

Now, let's get to the real deal—advanced goal setting. Goal setting needs to be done on your own time and on your own accord. The 'goals' set as part of your annual performance review are insufficient to truly be constructing your own career because you'll find they're purely focused on job performance. The issue with setting goals is you can't expect your performance reviewer or given mentor within an organisation to know how to set goals like this themselves. Take a step back and review the quality of their career and life. If it isn't exemplary and holistic, then should they really be imparting goal setting advice with you? I experienced a situation where a manager once deemed a small administrative item as part of my overall role to be considered a goal. I couldn't even fathom a response on the spot how small that was to even be considered a goal, let alone one that would contribute to career development. It just goes to reinforce who you generate and discuss goals with makes a big difference on the level of your achievement. If you don't do the internal work which was discussed at the start of the book, you'll forever be led by people with mindsets that only know how to think small and play safe.

"A goal properly set is halfway reached."
Zig Ziglar

I am sure you have heard of SMART goals, and this is also a practical application for goal setting. What it doesn't determine is the goal which will spur on greater progression. SMART goals miss the context of goal setting, and in isolation, don't take you far enough. There is an ABC goal model introduced by Bob Proctor, co-founder of the Proctor Gallagher Institute, on how you should set your goals. It splits goals into A-type, B-type and C-type.

A-type goals are goals you have already done before and ones you are well-versed in knowing how to achieve. These are goals that will keep on delivering the same standards and results you have already been achieving. For example, an A-type goal may be to ensure you get your 5% pay rise per year.

B-type goals are goals which you haven't done before, yet it's not something that will cause you to question whether you can achieve them. They're still a level up from A-type goals. For examples, you may want to buy a house. If you've never bought a property before, you'll figure out the processes and requirements to do so. If your goal is to then buy another house, this then becomes an A-type goal.

C-type goals is the arena you want to play in. C-type goals are goals you haven't done before and ones you also aren't sure yet, from your starting position how you'll achieve them. By all external measures, they don't need to be realistic. Your C-type goal is the goal you want the most, and will have unwavering resilience, persistence and motivation to achieve against everything else. A C-type goal could be starting a business or wanting to become a company director by the age of 30.

One of my C-type goals is to be a recognised international speaker. I haven't done this before. I haven't yet made association with people who run international events, and construction contexts are different around the world. But I know with absolute surety that this will happen, and every speaking engagement I undertake locally is drawing me closer and closer to achieving that.

C-type goals must tie back to your plan and your career brief. Now you know why you must achieve these goals; you'll have no issue raising your level of ambition and obsession to make it a reality. All the rubbish you've been telling yourself about why you shouldn't achieve your goals will dissipate, because the underlying reason is strong. Around 90% of my goals are C-type, and I use A and B to either maintain results in facets of my career and life, or to incrementally grow certain facets.

Now you have context for your goals and can reach and expand for more. With C-type goals, it's important you aren't solely focused on how it will be achieved. When you place too much emphasis on the how, you'll get into a state of disbelief and convince yourself they won't come into fruition. You need to focus on the why, with intense feeling, and knowing it will come true, and the how reveals itself. People, projects and opportunities will come your way that you either didn't see previously or have newly entered your life. That's exactly what happened to me once I set C-type goals tied to my vision. A whole new world of 'how' opened itself up to me.

There are elements of the SMART framework for goal setting which need to be adopted that will help you translate your C-type goals into detailed and actionable ones. I break this framework down as follows:

- **Specificity:** you can say you want to be a great project manager, but that's not specific. Your goals must be specific.
- **Measurable:** progression towards your goal need to be tracked, because the process in which you are applying to get your goal will be highly influential in whether you'll achieve it.
- Instead of achievable, I replace this with **actionable:** the steps to achieve that goal must be immediately actionable otherwise it will become

easy to forgo and do it "later" which can ultimately never come.

- **Results** – how do you know you have achieved a goal? If you were to relay your goal to someone else and told them you achieved it, would they concur? You must know exactly what it is you're seeking to attain from implementing your actions to support this goal.And finally,

- **T – time** is always of the essence. You can say you want to become a project manager, but by when? When your goal is not time-bound, there is no urgency, and with no urgency, there is little emotional action attached to it. If you want to be a project manager by the time you are 30, then 30 it is.

This planning and goal setting exercise is a continuous one. Just like a construction project; you're always planning, you're always aligning your activities to the bigger picture, and constantly revisiting to see what's working and what isn't. This isn't a set and forget exercise, but now you've learned how to set goals in context, you'll be able to effectively do so throughout your entire career.

"I am here for a purpose and that purpose is to grow into a mountain, not to shrink to a grain of sand. Henceforth will I apply all my efforts to become the highest mountain of all and I will strain my potential until it cries for mercy."
Og Mandino

PART THREE
CONSTRUCTION PHASE

FOUNDATIONS

"Skill is the unified force of experience, intellect and
passion in their operation."
John Ruskin

The skillset you bring to the marketplace is important to set strong foundations to your career moving forward. Even though skillset accounts for a low percentage towards long-term career success, that doesn't mean you have underdeveloped skills. Especially as you are playing in the professional market where the median level of performance is average. Having high-performance skills and attitude will always propel you to doing well, regardless of what you do. It is also your original skillset which determines your level of remuneration. It is all too commonplace for people to demand additional remuneration and benefits but can't add more value or deliver outstanding results because they never do any work on themselves.

Let's get one thing straight. Your employer isn't to blame if you consider yourself to be underpaid. The marketplace or the industry you are in (construction, in this case) is what places the value on your skill set. That's why executives who can make tough decisions fast are paid more than someone in administration who is performing repetitive data entry tasks. When it comes to remuneration, people lose their bearings quickly and are quick to compare, blame and contrast rather than make their income their own problem to solve. Therefore, the employer is just the vehicle in which your salary and income comes through from the marketplace. How you position and respond to the marketplace is what will dictate results. But it is not about upskilling yourself to attain the highest-paid position or follow the money. This all has to be in total alignment with all the inner work, design and programming you have been undertaking. See now why a career is such a fine craft, that not many ever bother to get right? Because it's a deeply thought out process. Your skill set is intrinsically tied to determining the amount of remuneration you attract, and the brilliant thing about this is you can improve the performance of your skill set to attract better pay.

Your employer has fundamentally hired you to increase the revenue, profitability and contribute to the overall growth of the business. You're there to continuously solve problems of varying magnitudes for the business on a day-to-day basis. If you're a Project Manager, your problem is how to deliver a project against given parameters and your solution will be a mix of people and processes to get you there. This comes with a skill set deemed to be more valuable to a business than someone in accounts. It is not that the accounts role is lesser or greater than a Project Management role, but they deem the inherent skills as more valuable by the marketplace which therefore attracts higher remuneration. This doesn't mean you are bound by a position and the pay. It is an opportunity for you to consider opportunities to introduce and implement more valuable skills into your position. If you are not making enough money in your position, it's a reflection of the quality of thinking and ingenuity going on in your mind. Why is it that a large significance of this book is about mindset and thinking? Because it's the activity that is undertaken the least.

To assess your current skill set, consider the following:

1. The more generic your skill set, the less money you will make.
2. The simpler the tasks you resolve in the workplace, the less money you will make.
3. The easier it is to replace you, the less money you'll make.

As a construction industry professional, what are then the high-income and high-performance skills you not only need to verse yourself in, but also master? Remember, you'll be working in both the social age and fourth industrial revolution which is fast approaching, if not in part already here. Let's start with complex problem solving.

A career in construction inherently develops this high-income skill as baseline problems involve cost, time, safety, quality and stakeholder consideration. When you can solve more and more complex problems, you will get paid for your results, not your time. Consider a specialist service consultant who can charge onwards of a few hundred dollars per hour. You're not paying the consultant for the time, but for their value to solve complex commissioning programs, for example. A workplace that will become more complex requires critical thinking. We develop this framework of thinking through mindset training and actual experience as it involves analysis, interpretation, inference, explanation, and problem solving.

Collaborative approaches of project management (in any capacity) is not only an afterthought but the basis of delivering outcomes. This isn't about saying 'let's all work together'; it involves understanding how to attain and maintain ongoing buy-in and focus from all project stakeholders and maintaining focus on the outcome of the project as an entity. External to the project management context, collaboration is required as a buy-in an involvement from multiple disciplines and departments is now becoming the norm. Being able to coordinate your work on the whole with others is imperative and requires a high level of organisation.

Self and social awareness is necessary in the social age when it is known what matters is who you are and who knows you. Failing to employ a heightened sense of awareness to the contexts you operate in will render you unable to effectively lead.

This makes leadership an essential skill. (It's more an attribute but is worthy of being on the list.) If you want results, you need to get the people who can make that happen with you, come with you. Leadership is a loaded concept and will be discussed in depth in the 'Management' chapter.

The ability to make decisions is a non-negotiable. Indecision adds to fear and doubt, which is already the natural operating state of many. When a decision is made, everyone can then proceed and work towards an outcome, but without a decision, work is suspended in motion and starts speculation within teams. An inability to make a decision shows a lack of confidence and ability to progress.

Creativity is not just an artform, but a demonstration of

coming up with ingenious solutions and ideas. It also shows maturity in your thinking as you can come up with ideas that are not solely based on past thinking. It might be completely new and novel ideas, or an application of ideas that have worked in parallel industries into construction. Interdisciplinary knowledge is when you combine frameworks from two unrelated industries to create something by blurring boundaries and is also a valuable form of creativity.

Interpersonal connectivity will lean on your ability to generate authentic human connections. In a world that is highly digitised, automated and isolated, the impact and worth of human connection will be highly valued. Undertake an assessment now of how many people in your workplace can foster such a human connection. Not many, right?

Not to be underrated, but time management is critical to high-performance skills. You may be a master of a certain aspect, but if it takes you double the time to achieve, is that really providing the best solution? Time management reflects your ability to organise, prioritise and manage the most important and finite resource—time. You can also take a step back and see how this skill is revered. How often are you amazed at what someone can achieve in a given period?

And finally, entrepreneurship. This is a stretch to consider it a skill set, it is more a skill category. I must include it as it covers initiative, innovation, resourcefulness, curiosity, courage, business and financial acumen and market knowledge—to name a few. This isn't to say you must become an entrepreneur or an intrapreneur, but that doesn't mean you can't think like one.

The list is over and above basic skills such as communication, emotional intelligence, negotiation, marketing, and the like, which form part of a basic toolkit you need as a professional.

And it is also not exhaustive. If anything, it should instigate your curiosity further to understand ways in which you can prime your skill set to match the demands of future markets to attract the high remuneration you desire. If there was still any doubt if the academic system really prepares you for the future of work, you can hopefully see by now it doesn't. The way they structure the learning and content doesn't develop any of the high-income skills required for your career. There should also be little to no doubt left in your mind that the onus to develop all this is on you. If you won't spend your resources of time and money to develop this, then you can also not expect your employer to pay you more than the minimum. Beforehand I also made the case for parallel careers. Well, now you can also see why this is required, because your direct line of work may not yield the opportunity to develop, say, complex thinking. But that doesn't mean the opportunity doesn't exist outside the workplace, you just have to seek it. If your excuse is you don't have the time or money to develop any of these skills, you'll be left behind. If you can't buy the book, go to a library. Listen to a podcast when you are commuting. Engage with a mentor who has all this. Go to a conference. The options today are unlimited. If you had to, you can offer a service of value in exchange for the one you are after. There is no lack of resources, only a lack of resourcefulness.

Salary

*"Don't think money does everything or you are going
to end up doing everything for money."*
Voltaire

It wouldn't be a book about careers without a discourse on salary. To my amazement, as I was researching aspects of this book and taking a high-level look at the career-related literature, there was little that integrated money mindset into constructing a career. Yes, there is a plethora of literature on discussing pay negotiations, pay review, pay equity, all of which comes into the conversation, but not the fundamental wiring associated with money. First, let's get rid of the stigma we want money. Of course, we want more money, it's not a bad thing. If we are trading our most valuable resource of time, then you want to be maximising the amount you get remunerated for it. There are too many negative connotations around desiring more money, which reflects the broken mindsets and flawed relationships people have with money. When you think of money, what are some first thoughts and beliefs that come up? Is it "money is the root of all evil?" "Money is not that important." Or "The rich get richer, the poor get poorer?" With these limiting, negative beliefs, how do you want more money to come into your life? You don't even need to look far, but how often in your circle is money openly discussed with good energy? Rarely, if ever. Yet this is the mindset people then seek higher compensation, added bonuses, and desire wealth in their life.

This is foundational knowledge, because you can't traverse your career, which is the primary vehicle for creating income with a mindset that is broken and flawed. Working in construction ruins your money mindset. We're actively taught to get the cheapest, bid to be the cheapest, and value economy over quality and solutions. They teach us to operate under a modality there is not enough money, and this reinforces a scarcity-based framework. You can't say having an abundance mindset in business doesn't result in financial success, because there are many organisations that operate under the principles of abundance that are wildly successful. Unfortunately, these money practices, of scarcity and constantly looking for a damn discount, then translate from one's professional life into their personal life. They continue to operate under a frequency of lack. This goes against our natural frequency of abundance.

There is abundance, no pun intended, of literature exploring your money mindset and your relationship with money. But your money mindset will be a massive factor in determining the amount of money that comes through the marketplace to you. It will also allow you to expand your possibilities to see money is a by-product of your value proposition to the market and you can control that. In turn, controlling the amount of money that comes to you. But you have to think of your career as a route to attract money to create the life and lifestyle you desire. This is why I had you again, do the inner work up front of figuring that all out. If you wished for a life of holidays whenever you wanted, multiple seven-figure wealth and financial freedom, I'd say you need to start your own business to remove the ceiling on your income or become an exceptional investor. (This is not financial or business advice.) If you were to say you wished for financial security, then a high-paying position where you are future-proofed will align just fine. What is important is you understand the life you desire has a price tag associated with it, and you need to consider if your career path aligns with it. This is why the programming work you did matters. If you identified you wanted to retire at forty, it's insufficient to have a salary that will not exceed six figures. Does this mean you chase the money? Not if it leaves you devoid of passion and purpose. Can you monetise your passion? Absolutely. Can you control and influence your skill set to ensure it aligns with high-income demands of the market? Of course you can. This is the foundational work you must build your career on. You can have the greatest looking building, but if the foundations are weak from the outset, then anything you ever build on top of it will only crumble and fall.

The construction industry actively rewards people who jump organisation by facilitating a 20-30% pay rise, if not more. This is how some attain high salaries quickly, but at some point, without adding more value, they price themselves out of the market. It's also common to see people take a position elsewhere for a mere $5,000 or $10,000 increase and sometimes leaving good organisations behind. Don't be blinded by short-term gain and be willing to forgo long-term objectives for little benefit if a move is purely fiscal. You have a lifetime to make an income.

When it comes to negotiating your pay, I will impart this with you. When you do all the development on yourself that has and is continuing to be discussed in this book, seeking higher compensation isn't such a daunting experience anymore. The first pitfall people have in the conversation of reviewing pay is they expect additional remuneration for the work they have already completed. It is important to relay your highlight reel and achievements, but not to expect more pay for what has already been done. What this serves to build is your future value. When you are pitching for a pay increase, you need to base it on your future value and all the results you will deliver. You need to become more to get paid more, it's simple. The second pitfall people make in this process is when asked why they deserve additional pay, is to recount personal considerations which have nothing to do with the business. Is your employer really concerned about saving up for your next holiday? Probably not. You are getting paid in exchange for the value you bring to the business, not for the value the business brings to you.

I have discussed skills and salary as foundational to your career, but there is one more part. I have made the case for personal development, and I've also made the case for professional development. But in construction, there is one more sphere you need to verse yourself in within the construction industry. And that is the construction industry itself. Let's say you are an industry professional who is working at one company and that is all you have ever known. The only thing said employee knows is the systems and processes and experienced passed through within that specific company. In your construction career, the only thing you get exposure to simply cannot be what you focus on within your position or only learn via experience. Nor should your research and expansion about the industry cease once you commence work. If you want to move faster in your career, you also have to learn faster about the industry, and you do this via full immersion. One of the CEO's I interviewed on my podcast has weekly conversations with other industry leaders to talk about the status of the industry, what's happening in the markets, what each company is doing. This gives them over time such an in-depth perception of what is happening in the industry that undoubtedly makes them a 'go-to' person within their domain and discipline. You can also do this as you can read the latest white papers, the latest blogs, the latest articles. You can take industry specific knowledge training courses. If you don't, then it takes twice as long to piece together the fabric of the industry. Via leaning into the experience of others, across all disciplines and companies, you're creating solid foundations to the wealth of industry knowledge. A site manager I used to work with did this and became a walking encyclopedia of anything to do with construction. He was extremely well-versed in project finances even though conventionally that doesn't fall under their "job description". He did this by taking a vested interest out of his own accord, even though it wasn't a direct job deliverable. By doing so, he positioned himself as being indispensable because of his knowledge and insight into everything.

Regardless of your position, you cannot have a telescopic view of the industry purely via one company and one position. Via the avenues suggested above, expand your repertoire of construction industry knowledge. Even spending one hour a week accumulated over years will position you above the competition as your career progresses. Don't underestimate how much you can learn about another company by talking to someone else, or how quickly your insight builds by actively seeking industry-based knowledge. This isn't studying, this isn't a call to undertake a degree. It is a call to continue engaging with the industry as a whole, so you don't only have one world view of how it works. Verse yourself in risk management, business and project governance, financial management, business development. In anything you do, know your numbers. When I was first passed this advice, it didn't come with context, but I understood it well later. In any position you are in, whether it's on a project or within a business, or any sector within the construction industry, know the finances, the numbers, like the back of your hand. You don't just arrive at an upper management position never having understood what the numbers mean now, and for the future of a business. We make important decisions about businesses by understanding the numbers, so you must do so too.

What would be the consequence if the only aspect of this book you adopted was the foundational stage? Are you thinking you'll be just fine in your career if you bypassed all the internal work and just did one aspect of it all? In that case, you're choosing to be great at your job rather than having an exceptional career, one you have constructed by strategic design. What comes before you start your footings on site? It's all the groundwork, of course. It's planning and designing. In the context of people, well, it results in the people who you will come across in your professional capacity and think, that's average. They're the people who live for the weekend. They only work to make a living, who won't go past the parameters of their position because it's not part of their job description. I have always been highly conscious of these sayings and challenge them, because if you don't then you adopt the psyche of the masses.

There is one thing you must exercise when building your foundations and it is this: patience. American author Joyce Meyer notes, "Patience is not simply the ability to wait - it's how we behave while we're waiting." One of the most common lessons parted on my podcast, Constructing You, is having patience is absolutely key. Being impatient can be quitting too soon, when your results were just around the corner. Being impatient also reduces the joy in the processes and the work. Patience is certainly a virtue.

Solidifying the foundations to a career you'll not just love, but be obsessed with having, is a process that doesn't end. It contradicts real life foundation construction, which you can move on from. But you're in it for the long run, and the only way you can develop the skills, the mindset, the experience, the holistic industry knowledge, is with time. The time will go by anyway. You'll hit the five-year mark, ten-year mark, but that alone is not a marker of success. The irony is, is that when people want something to happen quickly, they spend a lot of time seeking shortcuts. That time spent looking for shortcuts is a waste of time and energy, when it should have been applied taking the route they wanted to avoid in the first place; the one requiring them to play the long-term game.

SUPER-STRUCTURE

"Talent wins games, but teamwork and intelligence win championships."
Michael Jordan

The construction and property industries are people industries after all. Except when we look at our built environment as the projects that have been completed, it is always the name of the company that gets promoted. Of course, every individual cannot be named if you were telling someone who built it. But there is not enough discourse on the importance of the people behind the project, from many perspectives, which was one of the fuelling ideas of my podcast. I have worked on projects that were on paper, difficult to say the least. Where everything could go wrong, it did, and then continued to go pear-shaped. But the people I worked with were all exemplary. Everyone wanted to come to face the battles of that project day in day out because of the strong leadership and ownership displayed by everyone on the team. To date, I still consider it to be one of my favourite projects to have delivered. Then, there have been projects where I have worked on that on paper, are considered to be 'career-defining', and are projects most people would yearn to get on. Yet the lack-lustre leadership team and lack of formative culture conducive to delivering exceptional results made facing that project day in and out nothing less than a chore. When I also reflect on conversations I've had with other people in the industry, there is a similar sentiment. They might start off with "the project is great, but..." and lead into a host of issues with the people behind the projects. I've also been in conversation with people working on your stock standard builds but have an incredible team in place. You just see them light up when they get to talk about it. The people behind the projects are the super-structural requirements to constructing your career. You've heard the colloquialism—you're the average of the top five people you spend your time with. Choose wisely.

You need to be as considerate and conscious as you can about choosing the people you want to work with. And you do this by being selective with the company you work for. You need to undertake a 360-degree review of an organisation before choosing to work there. There will be a certain level of limitation on how much you can garner before you get your feet under the desk. But the construction industry is notoriously small, and this is where you need to tap into your relationship equity to get this insight. Now do you see how important networking is? I can safely say with the couple of times I have transitioned, my due diligence of the company prior to joining has been accurate. This is due diligence, not analysis paralysis where you place yourself into a state of being unable to make a decision without perfect information. Just as a potential employer is vetting you, you need to be vetting the employer. This sounds simple, but it's imperative this is comprehensively done. Think of the sheer quantum of hours you spend with the people at work. It's less hours than you spend with family and significant others. If you made the choice to pursue a corporate career, then make sure what you desire is in full alignment with what the organisation can offer.

I am particular about the company I keep and am only interested in A-grade people. The following is my criteria, which I use when assessing organisations and what I also discuss with my clients when they are looking to transition or enter the industry and need to align with an organisation. This is over and above the project and position considerations that were previously discussed. Consider the following:

- Culture refers to the beliefs and behaviours that influence how a company's employees and management interact with each other and people outside of the business. It is also what is referred to when someone says, "It's how it's done around here." Culture is more than just how employees are treated and valued; it also reflects the acceptable level of performance within an organisation. There is a common need to want to work somewhere where the people you work with are like your family. Think about your family unit for a minute. Are they forcing you for growth, or are your ideas and ventures always met with some resistance? I'm sure you've heard the justification from your family that "We're only trying to protect you." Families are necessary for support, belonging and unconditional acceptance. And typically, that's what people look for in their work. But I challenge you to give up that notion, because going to work with a team that is like family is a comfort zone, and the most growth doesn't happen in your comfort zone. Instead, identify cultures that create high-performance teams, which are based on discipline, accountability, results-orientated, training, and coaching. Think elite sports level or a military outfit.

- The culture of an organisation is built upon its core values, and now you've done the work to identify yours, you should only work for organisations in total alignment with your values. I don't agree with core values being compromised in the workplace, because if you compromise on something as important as that, you'll set negative habits for yourself. Compromising will become easy for you. Instead of asking organisations to solely detail their values, have them provide examples of that. If flexibility is important to you, then see if there are staff who are job-sharing, working from home, or the like.

- Assessment of growth opportunities – just like the structure of the building, you want to keep on going up. This is not only upwards in terms of title; this is in holistic growth. There is no issue remaining in any position for a long period, as long as your growth and engagement hasn't stagnated and it's what you want. Growth opportunities isn't just in terms of pay and promotion either. Consider opportunities for internal collaborations and executing unique projects as they come up, and the ability to not just move up but moving across to add to your skills and experiences.

- Reputation is important, because you are now aligning your personal brand with the perceivable reputation of an organisation within the marketplace. If you have aligned yourself with an organisation that is, for example, notorious for cutting corners, mistreating contractors and delivering inadequate work, you will by default adopt the perception of this reputation upon yourself. It doesn't matter if a company has been around for a hundred years or one year, their reputation is imperative.

- Alignment of personalities and working environment – I couldn't operate in an environment that was casual. There is nothing casual about me. A laid-back, chilled out environment would be my nightmare; a lax environment doesn't suit me for a minute. Maybe you prefer a work-hard, play-hard environment, because of your personality. Maybe you need to work somewhere that is an innovation hub, because you are someone who is a creative thinker. The environment you're in has to compliment your dominant attributes, otherwise it will be a source of friction in the workplace, and you won't know why.

- The vision of the company is important too, as an aspect or the whole of their vision should align with yours, otherwise there is no point working there. If you don't believe in the direction and purpose of the company, then why would you work there? Can you work for an organisation where the sole function is to increase the profitability of the owners? Or are you looking for an organisation with societal contribution and responsibility? If you don't want to go where the organisation is going, don't work there. Or make it a known short-term arrangement within your career plan as you may want to work on a particular project the organisation has. The purpose of an organisation could be tied to your personal mission or to have an organisational mission that aligns with you.

- The organisation needs to have industry standard systems and processes. I am sure you don't want to be occupying your day to day with clunky systems and extremely manual processes. Your zone of expertise is not updating several excel sheets which don't talk to each other. Systems and processes are there to make your day to day easier and freeing you up for the work that matters.

I want to debunk one further typical criterion people base their assessment of employers on. It's work-life balance. Work-life balance is a fallacy and is a social construct. I actively don't believe in it. It's become such the buzzword that few people stop to deconstruct it. The concept itself suggests balance, meaning that work and life are to be in total equilibrium. There are 168 hours in a week; do you work for 84 hours? If you subscribe to work-life balance, it suggests you should be working more. Imagine that life on a daily occurrence. How boring! What makes life is the ebbs and flows, the downs which makes the ups even better. To have a work-life balance, in my opinion, is to just flatline. The term to replace work-life balance is flexibility, but even so, we already have a level of flexibility in our employment arrangements; you're not expected to work 24/7/365 are you?

We live in a world of infinite potential and with the right mindset, strategic planning, mentoring and massive immediate action, we can achieve anything. People are so easy to make the call 'owning a business isn't for everyone' but you never hear anyone say that a 'corporate career isn't for everyone'. And it's usually the people who are sitting on the sidelines making that call. Some people don't want to climb the corporate ladder, they want to own it. There are many motives for starting a business; creating a vehicle to reclaim your time and build the lifestyle you want, seeing a gap in the marketplace, fulfilling your own potential. There is a reason I bring on as many founders of a business onto my podcast as possible, because I have to show you what is possible. There is a concept called belief transference; when you see people repeatedly creating something out of nothing and believing in themselves, their vision and pursuing their passion, you are more inclined to do the same; business or otherwise. Because you just start priming your mind to understand if it is possible for people no more extraordinary than you to do it, then you can too. Venturing out on your own is required when the only company you can see yourself working for is your own. The idea, or the itch to start a business, suggests you have untapped potential. Not everyone has this calling within or ambition, and of that, an even smaller percentage follows through and become successful. It was important in the discourse of constructing careers that not only a corporate one is presented as it would be limiting to suggest as such.

Additional members

"The road to success is always under construction."
Lily Tomlin

You're allowed to pivot and change, add to the plan, identify greater purposes. It's allowed to be a continual process of discovery as to keep building the structure. The structure is essentially everything you keep adding on to it to have a career. Build as large, as high and as wide as you want. What can frequently happen is you made a decision at a point in time based on the thinking you employed at the time. Remember, we live from the inside out. And then you arrive at your destination, and it's just not quite all that. It's not working for you, it's not making itself out to be all that, even though at the time the opportunity was aligned. You will experience points in time in your career where you need to transition, either into other sectors, disciplines, or companies, or because an opportunity has come up that aligns with your brief and design. Organisations also change, in terms of management, security, reputation, and that typically instigates movement.

It's common in the workplace to purposely jump from organisation to organisation to increase pay by 20-30%. As such, a jump year on year staying within one organisation is rare. The industry rewards this behaviour by offering far more attractive salaries if you jump, but money should not be the sole motivator for moving. If there is an opportunity aligned with your brief, design, your purpose, or you have buy-in into the purpose of the organisation, which requires a pay cut, it may well be worth it. It can look like taking two steps forward one step back. Moving up and around in terms of higher salary is an external trapping of success.

FAÇADE

"If you want to be seen, you have to put yourself out there - it's that simple."
Karin Fossum

Talent isn't the issue. Obscurity is. You can be the absolute best, but if the right people aren't seeing that, you're not moving fast enough in your career. If hard work was the sole predictor to career success, then you should be able to work twenty-four hours a day at your job and get all the pay and all the promotion. Physical labouring would be the most revered position, if hard work was the case. And if your sole value proposition is hard work, remember someone else can always outwork you as there is no ceiling to how hard someone can work. Alas, none of this is the case. Nor is it sufficient to do the minimum requirements of your job, and possibly stay there for long enough and expect pay rises and promotion to come your way. If you do, then you fall into the category of an average professional, and I am sure if you are reading this book, your goal is to be exceptional. When you get comfortable and complacent, remember this:

- Does anyone owe you anything?
- Do you expect reward and recognition based on presenteeism and tenure?
- Do you put in the minimum but want the maximum?

If you answered yes to any of the above, you haven't taken full agency of your career and aren't in a positioning of propelling, but rather, digressing.

Networking is one avenue in which you get seen, and I previously discussed how you can work to raise your profile via networking, which has its advantages. The only limitation of physical networking is that it is time consuming and you have to physically (or virtually) be in attendance somewhere, and at times there is a financial investment that goes with it. But this is where the power of social media comes in to play. We have at our disposal one of the most powerful professional building tools that also happens to be free. I love LinkedIn. I have an honest and legitimate love for this platform, because of the career benefits it yields.

Prior to my more prolific usage of LinkedIn as an industry leader, I was a mild user at a time when not that many construction industry professionals were online. I still find an outdated psyche in the industry, where people expect their tenure, hard work and also projects to speak for themselves. How? How will that be the case? It won't. I would go to industry events and post a photo of the event (never of me) with a recap why I enjoyed it and what

I learned from it. I then started posting about work or personal related events, such as winning the Young Achiever of the Year Award for my excellence on project delivery. Or graduating from my Master of Construction Management, in amongst other things. And this was never in the intention of attaining employment or getting leads. I was sharing it with the community because it meant something to me, and it was important to bring people along that journey. In between posting, I would engage with other's content, albeit infrequently compared to now. Going on LinkedIn was just what I did whenever I'd an interesting experience to share. Little did I know I was consequentially establishing a brand and recognition all along. I know this is a huge cornerstone of my online presence and success of today, but it is just another example of doing the work and playing the long-term game. Remember, the day you plant the seed is not the day you eat the fruit.

Even as a result of my intermittent posting of experiences and wins during my first five years of my career, I was constantly attracting opportunities. Until I figured out you could switch off the marker to let premium profiles know you weren't open to opportunities, I would get at least one a week. I would get approached more frequently than not if I was interested in 'having a coffee' to meet someone in a company that was looking to hire. At first, I was perplexed, and asked around about the volume and frequency, and few had a similar experience. I was being *seen*. It wasn't just commentary from people outside the organisation I was working at, it was also people *within* the organisation that were seeing, complimenting, interested, in what I was doing outside of work. I realised then that being seen is imperative to accessing opportunities. This comes with people who have other ideas. You need to realise no one will do your own self-promotion for you. I have always been under the frame of mind that if I don't do it, no one else will. It is highly unlikely your boss, HR, partner, best friend, will write up a post every time you achieve something, have an article to share, or the like. Sure, you get a tag here or there, but that isn't enough to open the flood gates of opportunities you need to construct your career. Remember, your career is a business. What is the point of having a business if no one knows you are open for business, or are a key player in the market and here promote your services? The intention is to get headhunted, not go hunting for opportunities. You know you're piecing it all together when hiring managers and recruiters are knocking on your door.

I won't discuss Instagram or other social platforms as each has a unique purpose. Studies have found when a person searches for another on social platforms and nothing shows up, trust is automatically broken. It is known people are also likely to be overlooked for interviews without an online presence. Think about your own behaviour; whether it's a dating app match or the person walking into the interview room, you've searched for them online. How disappointed were you that your search yielded outdated or irrelevant information about the person? Before you have even spoken to that person, you have preconceived and predisposed notions about them, purely based on a five second online search. We are living in the social age today. The industrial age is gone, the information age is gone, and it's the social age powered by presence, visibility and connectivity which dominates. I would even go so far as saying it is negligent practice to not have an online presence. If you're not establishing your online presence now, it is only getting empirically noisier and difficult, especially once algorithms change. The organic reach at the time of writing is unlike any other platform. Building a digital footprint creates presence and visibility in a professional community and works to highlight your expertise in a field has more weight on it than ever before.

Think about your own habits. When you want to purchase something online, you search for it, read the reviews, maybe watch a few videos. You're looking for validation this is the right purchase. It is no different to people of decision-making capacity in an organisation doing the same when reviewing prospective employees for opportunities. Except, unlike Google Reviews where you can't really stop a bad review from being posted, you have full agency and control over your LinkedIn profile. I think of your profile as your house. When you invite someone over, what do you want them to see? A mess, with seven weeks' worth of laundry piled high? And a project you started but never quite finished sprawled over the dining room table? Unlikely. You want to present an immaculate front that shows off every best feature of your house. You do this with your profile by having it constantly completed and up to date, but also active at a minimum. If your last engagement was months ago, that again breaks the trust. But your profile is a walking billboard of not just what you do, but who you are. You can have a profile on par with industry professionals which is heavily based on their technical capacity, but this is insufficient to keep eyes on the screen. Again, look to your own habits. How quickly do you scroll over a post, maintain engagement? Not long. Your profile needs to have insight into who you are. This does not mean naming your favourite hobbies and favourite restaurant. It means highlighting your core attributes and values, and that can be displayed in your biography, in your features section, and in showcasing work and activity you do outside of work. People who have this kind of information available on their profile not only perform better in terms of search metrics but achieve what needs to be achieved—visibility!

LinkedIn is a double-edged sword. To be seen, you have to both add value and engage. I like to think of LinkedIn as a global networking event that never goes to sleep. What's your approach? Are you going to be a wallflower? Are you going to only hang out and talk to your friends and the people you work with? That is not the point of having access to anyone in the world that has a profile. The more you engage with the people you want to get in front of, the more of a relationship you are inherently creating. And the benefit of such a platform is this happens concurrently with hundreds, if not thousands of people. If you comment again and again on the content of a person you want to get in front of, they'll see you. For example, my social profiles have amassed over five figures of connections, but the ones I remember are the ones who consistently engage with my content. Take note the content has to be great in the first place for them to do so. Just because you think the content is great, doesn't mean it is. When you create content, you have the opportunity to constantly show up in the feed of people in your network. Content strategy and formulation is a topic within itself, but there is nothing stopping you from posting about your recent award win, a project you are working on, an event you went to. Have a look at your life to realise the content is all already there, it just needs to be captured. At the same time, be considerate of outdated content you probably don't want future employers discovering. Discretion is necessary at times.

Do you see how this puts you ahead of the competition? Because you are inadvertently putting yourself front and centre and consistently so in front of the decision makers and people with opportunity. This is the façade you are presenting to the industry, but the façade only gets installed after the super-structure. (To all you technically minded readers, yes, I am aware of staging.) You need to first understand the structure of your career, what you're here to do exactly, before you can present that to the industry. What I find is many people do that backwards. They'll put out arbitrary comments or content just to see what sticks or do something for the sake of doing it. But if you do this all correctly, you're reaching people every day where their eyes are. On the screen. I find this is even more pressing to project teams who have no direct daily presence with upper echelon positions within the company they work for.

For example, you're a superstar of a Project Coordinator based out on site. You have the talent, that shows, and your team thinks you're doing a great job. But if your sole strategy is to rely on your Project Manager to make sure the Construction Manager sees that; you're creating unnecessary risk to your career. There are far and few managers who surpass management level into leadership and want others to succeed more than them. Nor should you solely rely on the annual performance review to demonstrate your talent, because a whole year has gone in between, and people are forgetful of all the brilliant work you did. But when you take that scope of works, and team it with other attributes of your career and put it online, you're gaining visibility. I've met people at corporate functions and gatherings I am only connected with online who knew all about what I have done, been featured in. Yet we've worked in the same organisation for two years and we've never met in person. That is a consequence of a large organisation. But even within smaller organisations, wouldn't you want your boss to come to you and see your work for what it is? That is the power of social media.

But what is this really working to build? Surely not just a digital footprint? No, it's much larger than that. What having a digital footprint does is control the brand around your name. You get to control what is and isn't said about your name. You must always take ownership about the content posted online and be able to back it up. People can see right through lack of authenticity or false claims and the like. That will do you no justice. Your brand is far more than just a colour palette you think suits the industry you're in. Far from. A brand is a complex piece of construction that takes years to develop and seconds to deconstruct. Think of a façade, how all the parts so coherently go together, that you just can't imagine them being put together any other way. That's your brand. It's a perfect piece of architecture and construction coming together that when someone drives by, they get a sense of who you are and what they can expect. This is by no means an instruction for you to go out and get a designer to detail a brand for you. A brand is more than just a visual; it is a way of life, a way of being consistent through and through in any application. A personal brand is a key requirement for differentiation and marketing yourself how you desire to be seen and heard. Having a personal brand allows others to consistently see and reinforce who you are and what it is you are here to do, in your career and your life. When someone says your name when you're not in the room, what should they be saying?

The first part in which people falter when creating a personal brand to stand out is never having done a mix of the foundational and structural work of understanding who they are. They have fallen in line with the identity of the job title and continue to carry that and let that override. I have seen site managers who have "had to be" more aggressive and adversarial because the nature of the project demanded it (which is only an inaccurate perception). I have seen Project Managers demonstrate zero emotion, because somewhere along the lines they were told to be cool, calm and clinical "to get the job done". Whereas they were far more people orientated than that. I have seen people take on aggressive demeanours because there is a common misconception about the person one should be to have a successful career in construction.

It is easy though to be so malleable to what other people say you have to be when you've never considered who you really are. Your professional identity is a long process of introspection unremoved from your personal one, and to instigate this, consider:

- What are my core seven values?
- What are my dominant characteristics?
- What level of performance do I value and operate at?
- What do people typically ask me for help or advice on?
- What do I stand for and be known for in my industry?

I know from having been through building mine, it is extremely considered, intensive, takes months to start up, and years to implement. These questions are only to bring to the surface the important and fundamental considerations about how you can start constructing this yourself. The question that has a lot of weight to it is what you want to be known for. This shouldn't come to you with great friction anymore because you have (hopefully) done the structural work involved. Having this as your plan will guide the development of your personal brand. It will also allow you to build on your professional reputation by engaging in roles and projects, both internally and externally to your organisation. This will strengthen the brand and identity of your name you are creating in the marketplace.

> *"All of us need to understand the importance of branding. We are CEOs of our own companies: Me Inc. To be in business today, our most important job is to be head marketer for the brand called You."*
> **Tom Peters**

Your personal brand further solidifies your visibility when you are a speaker or a panellist at industry events, and you position yourself as the 'go-to' person. When you are the recognised individual for being the expert on a particular topic and it becomes what you stand for, you are in a more premium position to attract higher remuneration. This could be anything from collaborative project delivery to construction technology. Certainly, you don't venture down a path that doesn't align with your passion and purpose because of prospective remuneration, but it is one of the consequential effects of having a brand versus not. Your brand is your reputation and the level of remuneration you attract because it reflects your strength or otherwise of your brand and positioning.

Branding is further exemplified by many other domains you need to appear in and share your perspective on what you want to be known for. If project management is your domain, contribute expert opinion articles to industry relevant publications. Contribute to a blog, a specific professional association. The avenues are endless. All this works to increase your visibility and crafting the message you want known about you in the industry. Remember though, you are not an expert on one single industry topic. I see it frequently where people spread themselves far too wide, positioning themselves as a jack of all trades, master of none. People need to quickly and clearly understand your brand, which is why your elevator pitch is important. When you meet someone, the first thing that needs to stop is to introduce yourself as your job title. I have never said "I am a Contract Administrator..." You're not a position. My response is who I am, and then in the mix, I used to say what I work as.

Your brand is also translated in the quality of work you do and your automatic, or default levels of operation. Are you someone who takes extreme ownership of their work, will never blame others, and demonstrates comprehensiveness and quality through and through? Or, do you do the minimum as required, and cannot wait for 4pm Friday beers? The aforementioned are two different people. Average is an acceptable standard in society as a whole, and people get away with it all the time. Being average is when you validate you should leave work early because you stayed late two weeks ago. Average is validating stealing stationary from work because you pay for the fuel to come to work. Average is not following a process in its entirety because everyone else does it that way. Do you see how easy it is for average performance to permeate your career too? We all know projects abide by standards. Why have our careers and performance become exempt from this? They haven't. If your brand and positioning is about being the best in a chosen sector or profession within construction, so must your standards. I will discuss high performance in the next chapter. If you are seen to be the ones raising the standards of your performance and your teams' performance, you can be guaranteed visibility and all the benefits that come with it too.

I remember once my friend in industry was telling me how she was catching up with people who knew who I was, but I'd no idea who they were. "Oh, we know Elinor Moshe." That is when you know your visibility has increased, but it is only at the effort of both online and offline presence. As Tim Ferriss quotes, "Personal branding is about managing your name — even if you don't own a business — in a world of misinformation, disinformation, and semi-permanent Google records." It is when people know who and what you are about just by saying your name. With every positive reaction there is an equal and opposite reaction. You will get a range of criticisms and people challenging you as you become more visible, but that should not deter you. There may be people in your organisation who have zero appreciation for everything you do. That can be a consequence of either your conveyance of the message or this isn't the right organisation for you. Like many projects, there will be twists and turns, challenges and concerns thrown your way.

It is up to you to consider and weigh up the risk of not having a digital footprint, online presence and personal brand to construct your career. I perceive the risk moving forward to be too great. You're right in thinking there are people who have successfully constructed their career without any of this, but you have to ask— will their career and business be future-proof? What they have done may have worked until now, but that is not a marker it will continue to work. You will realise you need the façade for every stage of your career and will pay the significant price in your career of not having it.

PART FOUR

OPERATIONAL PHASE

PERFORMANCE

*"Excellence comes from an internal standard that
asks, 'How can I deliver beyond what's expected?'"*
Brendon Burchard

Do you know who will impose high standards for your career
and life? No one except you. Who will push you on the daily to
maintain high standards of performance? No one except you. Do
you know who will hold yourself accountable to your own plans
and goals? You guessed it, it's you again.

Once you've finished this chapter, I'd like you to go into
work and make a mental checklist of who is a high-performance
individual in your workplace or project team. Have a close look
at their habits. I'm not just talking about the output of their
work. And high performance doesn't mean who is at the office
the longest. Average performance has crept its way through to our
careers and, inherently, life. The same ethos of my podcast applies

to my book. I want you to have an exceptional, exemplary, and excellent career in construction, and you're about to up your level of performance to do that.

High-performance individuals undoubtedly are the ones who progress faster and attain more recognition. High-performance individuals deliver more results in any given amount of time compared to the norm, and as Bill Parcells, head coach of the NFL said, "You don't get any medal for trying something, you get medals for results."

I frequently get asked, "How do I manage to do it all?" This was even the case before I founded The Construction Coach. Once upon a time it was full-time work on project delivery, completing my master's degree and volunteering for a not-for-profit association. Fast forward to launching and running my business, The Construction Coach, I get asked all the same. People who don't know the full extent of what I do may think it's just content creation, but it's far from that. I work in the business, on the business, and on myself, and delivering results and value to my clients and community, who come first and foremost. To me, it came easy adding in an extra moving part, and another, and another. When I wanted to start the podcast, all I heard were words of warning about how much time it will take, how complicated it is, so on, so forth. Had I heeded the advice from the podcasting community, I wouldn't have launched a podcast. But I have an ability to always make it work. And that's because for years I have developed high-performance habits that I apply myself where required to achieve what I need. And only because I have developed and proven high-performance standards for myself, can I demand them from others.

No one ever demanded this level from me; it's been innate but also driven by my ambition and determination. I have always been unwavering in pursuing my goals, and once I started getting results from my efforts... Let me tell you, it is addictive. But it is this level of operation, which is required to have a career you deserve, and to develop the muscle to do whatever it takes. To do whatever it takes requires a level of temporary sacrifice. Of foregoing short-term pleasure for long-term gain, and this I have no issue doing. American football player Jerry Rice said, "Today I will do what others won't, so tomorrow I can accomplish what others can't." This is why I had you, up front, determine what it is you want. Then, like me, you know what you're in pursuit of, and have ignited that internal force that will make sure you achieve and accomplish.

Just as you work out the muscles in your body, you need to work out the muscle in your brain to get them going. If you've never focused on deep work for more than ten minutes, it doesn't mean you're not good at it. It's just a sedentary muscle in the brain that needs work. I'll now give you insight into my top nine high-performance habits, starting with my favourite: focus.

I have a laser-like focus. When I set my mind to a goal, it's happening. My past performance has shown me this is the case. Anything I set my mind to comes into fruition. I just don't know when, but I also know when I've hung in there longer than I sometimes even wanted to, it's paid off. I focus only on my priorities; I don't have scattered focus because then nothing gets achieved. When you're focused, common issues like procrastination and distractions fall away. To write this book has taken my level of focus to a whole new level. The most detrimental thing to writing is to lose focus, because it takes additional energy to bring your focus back. Worse, losing your train of thought or that key concept or idea you want to convey in a particular matter. It's the same for when you are consumed in deep planning work or thought. Where people falter with focus is when their inner circle of family and friends start getting angsty and annoyed with them for being unavailable or saying no when they've previously said yes. They succumb again to the short-term pleasure instead of focusing on the long-term gain. There are many ways to train your brain to focus, and it can be as simple as committing to concentrating and finishing a book. (Hopefully this one.) Have a laser-like focus in everything you do, there is no other way.

Jim Rohn, American entrepreneur, author and motivational speaker said, "Discipline is the bridge between goals and accomplishment." Self-discipline is important when achieving career success and is a form of commitment. When I set a task for myself, I know I have a limited amount of time to get it done in, to the highest quality. Because if I slip and don't do it, I'm not doing my future self any favours. I experienced this well during my undergraduate degree. I didn't have the level of structure I now employ in my life. I was lax and free form, which meant a lot of late nights and starting essays forty-eight hours before they were due. When I went into my master's degree, I knew the same approach wouldn't work, so I employed stringent structures to my time. It helped build discipline to get it done, and I carried that same discipline to my projects. That's why when I need to add a business, a podcast, an event, a client, whatever it is; I have the discipline muscle sorted. What may also work for you is a reward. When you reward the performance you are seeking to achieve, you're cementing the habit and associating it with good things.

What fuels discipline, however, is accountability. Bob Proctor said: "Accountability is the glue that ties commitment to the result." If I promised a client a proposal in forty-eight hours, or that I would show up at 7pm for a session, it's happening. If I said I would respond with a submission in three days, it's happening.

That's to external parties, but with myself, if I say I will write 5000 words on the weekend, it's happening. Accountability is doing what you'll say. Next time you're not doing what you will say you will do, note the easy excuses and justifications that come up. What results have they been getting you? Surely not the ones you want. It's so easy in a professional context to say, "I forgot", "I didn't get a chance to…" and so on, but this is a low level of accountability. The goal posts can change, as they do, but then it becomes about managing people's expectations, because they get disappointed quickly, and build a subconscious perception about you. If you say you'll do it, to yourself or someone else, do it. It requires discipline to have consistency in action. If you only do the work you need to be doing for when you feel like it, you won't get much done. That is wholly operating out of your comfort zone, and we all know no growth happens there.

This leans into the zone of no excuses. I could easily come up with an excuse why I don't feel like creating content right now, why now isn't the great time to film, why now isn't the time, so on, so forth. But they are all just excuses, and on the high level is not the root cause why you're coming up with an excuse. For example, you may be putting off asking for a pay rise. The common excuses could be, "the boss is busy", "now isn't the right time". But all this could mask a fear of rejection, of failure, of feeling like you're not good enough if you don't get it. The excuses we can actively hear in our mind are only the surface level ones, not the root cause. Do what you need to do despite all your excuses, as do you need to get to the root cause of what is causing you to stall. Russian-American writer and philosopher Ayn Rand said, "Rationalisation is a process of not perceiving reality, but of attempting to make reality fit one's emotions."

In high school, I distinctly remember the teachers at parent-teacher interviews always saying, "What a hard-worker Elinor is." Yes, she is! Diligence is one of my strong suites, because I know the only way to achieve the goals I set is by doing the work involved. Benjamin Franklin said, "Diligence is the mother of good luck." It's essential to creating your own fortune. Nothing comes if you don't go out there and work for it. It is diligence tied in with all the other habits that will get you to new levels of accomplishment in your career. This applies to what you do inside and outside of work.

Because I need many moving parts to my life to maintain the level of results and motivation, I've also had to become highly productive. I am efficient, and I work fast. It's the culmination of discipline and diligence. Being able to manage your time to do what you need to do is a key high-performance habit. The people who have huge goals and visions are not lax with their time. British business magnate, investor, author and philanthropist Richard Branson is entitled to kick back on his island, but have you earned that luxury yet? Have you earned the luxury to do it tomorrow? I don't think so. Neither have I, yet. Is your career where you want it to be? I am sensitive where my time goes and can get irate when I feel it's wasted. The key way you'll attend to your key priorities is via time management, and then what you can do in that time. The details of productivity are really not sexy to talk about, but they're ultra-important and are core skills that will continue to serve you through every stage of your career.

I sincerely hope by this stage of the book you will realise the majority, if not all the requirements will involve your own self-directed learning. I only know a handful of organisations that actively promote high-performance habits and that's because I've interviewed them for my podcast. But your organisation won't take you by the hand, sit you down, and road map what you need to learn, will they? If you perceive your communication to be a weakness, read a communication book, take a course, hire a coach. If you want to become an excellent negotiator, you'll start learning human psychology. You want this brilliant career? You'll work on the greatest project of all. It's all on you. You must keep on learning. Canadian-American author and motivational speaker Brian Tracy said, "Continuous learning is the minimum requirement for success in any field." You have no choice in constructing your career to do this.

A reason I can move forward fast and propel myself towards achievement is my ability to take risks. I roll the dice. I don't hold the dice in my hands, scared I won't get a double six. I take the risk because I am curious as to the outcome, and I desire the result. Not just for me, for my community. Something as simple as putting on an event is a risk, but if I don't do it, I am not imparting the experience my community needs and solving their problems. It is only through the experiences of taking risks can you increase your performance. When you take the risk, you'll either learn or grow, and that's a win. Being risk-adverse will stagnate and stall you, fast.

And finally, high-performance individuals exercise this concept through and through. It's extreme ownership. Extreme ownership is a universal concept that has been more popularised in the book 'Extreme Ownership' by Jocko Willink and Leif Babin. Extreme ownership is about taking full, unwavering responsibility for everything that is happening in your world to the ultimate degree. It means you assume responsibility for the tasks which you can directly control, and for those you can't but have an implication to the success or otherwise of your mission. This is not a concept reserved for people in leadership positions. It applies to you from day one. Extreme ownership is never about passing blame onto a subordinate, because ultimately there is something you could have done differently to change the outcome. Displaying extreme ownership and always owning up to a situation displays intense integrity and trust. Jocko Willink and Leif Babin write, "Implementing Extreme Ownership requires checking your ego and operating with a high degree of humility. Admitting mistakes, taking ownership, and developing a plan to overcome challenges are integral to any successful team."

Anything worth having is not necessarily made easy. Kilroy J. Oldster, accomplished attorney reflects on this perfectly. "High performers whom exhibit tremendous self-control tend to be burdened by their own competence. Studies indicate that being extraordinarily competent can place a person under an unusual amount of stress because it raises other people's expectation of them. The more tasks an exemplary employee produces with a 'go-getting personality' while maintaining high quality relationships with peers and clients, the more an organisation underestimates their actual effort and the more it expects of them. Other people do not comprehend how difficult it is for a high performer to complete multifaceted tasks. They also tend to underestimate how much effort an enterprising person exerts who maintains a positive and pleasant attitude while completing difficult assignments."

I wanted to share this to quell your doubt, and know in becoming a high-performance individual, you'll face some friction and frustration. But it's your choice to be average or to be exceptional. I trust you'll choose well.

Performance reviews

*"If my future were determined just by my
performance on a standardized test, I wouldn't be
here. I guarantee you that."*
Michelle Obama

Could it be a career intelligence book without discussing performance reviews? One day I would like to think so, because it's a perfunctory piece in corporate careers which causes much undue stress for many. The performance review isn't the point in time in which career development happens. If you isolate your development to solely be around mid-year and around pay reviews, you're running a huge unnecessary risk. It is just one formal point in time in which obligations around your performance are met, and we've entered a few goals into the system with dates, long forgotten.It's important to remove the emotion attached to performance reviews. Quite frankly, you're on review every day, not just around performance time. And if you're the manager, you should be continuously providing feedback that is developmental and formative. Having your emotions in check during this feedback process is imperative to remove the undue negativity around it. It's important you place more emphasis on the preparation and the process rather than mulling over the outcome. Where people come up short during performance reviews is failing to take stock throughout the whole year of all the achievements, big and small. It is likely around performance review time, you and the reviewing party will recall all the big events that occurred. But when you add in all the small wins along the way, you're presenting the best business case for yourself. Use this time to remind the reviewing party of all the great work you've done. It can be a simple task of keeping a document on your desktop and logging all the wins by taking stock once a week. By the time your review comes around, I wouldn't be surprised if you won't have pages and pages of achievements, wins and successes. When you have such an accurate and detailed list that cannot be refuted, it sets a trend for yourself, which gives you a runway into asking for that additional pay or promotion. Ensure when your reviewing party provides feedback, positive or otherwise, it's always substantiated with evidence. All claims need to be backed up, especially if they are negative. It's insufficient from a management perspective to base a review on perception, feelings and hearsay. This opinion could be detrimental to future prospects if it is incorrectly fed up the line, so pushing to have the feedback based in fact and not fiction is imperative.

If the outcome of the performance review isn't what you anticipated, it could serve as another great prompt to check into where you are with your career. But do not rely on this annual event to do so.

And now you know what high performance really entails, make sure that that's what the review is against.

Professional Practice

"We are what we repeatedly do. Excellence, then, is
not an act, but a habit."
Aristotle

The high-performance habits you'll now dictate and demand from yourself is in relation to your personal development. In construction, there is also a level of minimum acceptable performance standards imperative to constructing your career that is industry specific. While it may be common knowledge, it's not commonly practiced.The first is you don't need to cheat, rip-off or short-change a contractor, client, or subcontractor to make a profit on delivery. Even if you're not planning to work directly on project delivery, understand decisions you make go down the line and have implications on contractors (head and subcontractors). This behaviour of being aggressive and adversarial towards trades especially is only a consequence of head contractors also entering into tight contracts with clients. The fragmented nature of the industry means competition is rife, and clients have options. So, to win a project in a competitive market, some builders go in on a negative margin, at cost, or with a tiny margin to win the project. To win this back, or even maximise the percentage of profit on a project, builders seek to get this back from subcontractors by either negotiating heavily at tender time. Or being unfair and "stitching up" subcontractors by not paying them or withholding money in some form. If you're wondering why cash retentions don't get released, it's likely being used as a cash reserve to fuel projects. This is a generalisation but also a cross-section of the industry. I hope one day this section of the book becomes outdated practice. Now head contractors and subcontractors are bound by a contract, and the contract is in place to protect both parties, so I think it's fair play both parties are to maintain and fulfil their contractual obligations. And when there is a breach, well the contract has certain mechanisms to protect both parties, and agreeably at times, they need to be used. I'm all for fair and reasonable practice, because you can't argue with something that is fair and reasonable, now can you?

But so many subcontractors go under because of bad business with builders. This is just one negative consequence of being such a cost-driven industry. We all want to pay fair market value for goods and services, no problem with that. Subcontractors are people too, with businesses to run and families to support. They're not greater than or lesser than a head contractor, we're all equal. There is this hidden mentality that subcontractors aren't entitled to profit or to be commercially savvy.

So many projects as an entity of their own suffer because people are conditioned along the way to work against each other rather than with each other, especially subcontractors.

Who told you the only way to achieve project success is to short-change the contractor, and even the consultant, and play the adversarial game?

Remember, construction is about building long-term relationships, and one day, you'll need a favour from a contractor, a client maybe. Do you think they'll jump for you if you've been horrible? No, they won't. It helps a lot when a contractor will ramp up their labour for you because they know you'll pay, for example. I'm pleased I have successfully delivered projects at a profit and have subcontractors who will happily price works for me and want to work on projects I am delivering because how firm and fair I am.

So, when you're entering industry, or are already there, and before you get conditioned to screw everyone down, think about this:

A collaborative framework to project delivery will maximise your success. Everyone can make money—the client, the consultants, the builder, the subcontractor, the supplier.

What we fail to realise in contracting is we have created another entity, and that is the project. The project suffers when everyone is literally playing games and looking to screw down anyone. Contractual claims can burden efficient collaboration in construction. I perceive a collaborative framework for project delivery is essential; let's have teams working towards a common goal and can all walk away with success stories rather than war stories. Let's rescind the adversary. It's a project environment I perceive as conducive to success and one I hope to see across all tiers of project delivery. Wouldn't that be a great future?

Collaboration in construction is not a soft approach to project delivery, but a project management framework that generates long-term win-win approaches to work. Collaboration is about building a relationship-centric approach conducive to trust, respect and meaningful communication, which improves results for all stakeholders.

This approach does away with the traditional arms' length relationships. It moves to ones based on equality and involvement, where it's clear from the outset everyone has the right to make a profit and contribute to the betterment of the project.

This approach can also turn conventional tendering practices on its head, whereby the cheapest price is always the winner. We must go to the market to achieve a competitive price, while wasting company resources in the process. I can't be the only one to consider tendering an extreme inefficiency of the construction industry.

At the end of the day, no one needs to go home with frustration or concerns about a poor performing project. Wouldn't you rather spend your time planning and thinking how can all parties move forward together rather than how can one party maximise their success at the expense of another?

MANAGEMENT

"Practice Golden-Rule 1 of Management in everything you do. Manage others the way you would like to be managed."
Brian Tracy

You're at the operational stage of your career now, and if you're reading this book, I know you have great aspirations and ambitions. You've built the foundations, you've constructed your super-structure, and you have a high performing building. Well, career. All this work cannot go unmanaged. Think of any project itself. What are the dire consequences when inputs and outputs go unmanaged? How quickly will everything veer off track? Fast.

There are two aspects to management of your career: management of yourself and management of others. We've already covered management of self in performance, so let's move on with management of others.

Developing your management style

*"Good management consists in showing average
people how to do the work of superior people."*
John D. Rockefeller

To avoid doubt, I'll say it again: the construction industry is a small industry built on relationships and connections. It's first and foremost a people industry; I really need you to understand that to construct your career. Where do opportunities come from? People. Where does money come from? People. Where does appreciation and recognition come from? People. Your reputation and your name precede you faster than you can imagine because of the dense and close networks in each market sector.

In every capacity in your career, people will be involved along the way to you achieving your end goal. You have two options: you can work with the person or work around them. Because of the transient nature of projects, you'll be working with more people than if you worked in a conventional office position where the number of people you have exposure to is limited. Well, you have a third option of walking away, but I won't put that on the table because it's not always an option in the context of employment.

A senior site manager I worked with had a developed and mature talent of figuring people out within the first few minutes of meeting them. What that allowed was for him to integrate his approach and communication to suit the individual to get them to work with his objectives. Reading people and understanding their game and objective is key to your career success. Everyone is different and you need to deal with people in a different manner without compromising your management style. In the construction game, it's preferable to have people on your side. This is great when you can work with the person. But there are many personalities in the industry—I don't even need to look that far—within a project. There will be times when you will have to work around someone to meet your own objectives. You can still work with the hardest and meanest construction types in industry and come out strong. It all falls to figuring out the person in a matter of minutes, and your ability to read others will greatly impact how you will deal with them and vice versa.

"If you pick the right people and give them the opportunity to spread their wings—and put compensation as a carrier behind it—you almost don't have to manage them."
Jack Welch

Second to this, you need to develop your own style of managing people, and this is a chance to install uniqueness within yourself. The same ethos applies for leadership which will be discussed further on in this chapter. In the early days of your career, you'll first observe the management styles of others and mirror the behaviour of your immediate management team, for better or for worse. I'll refer back to the aforementioned site manager. He was known for being firm, fair and reasonable, which established great relationships with the subcontractors. The subcontractors knew his agenda was for project success and he wouldn't be achieving that via compromising the subcontractors. As a result, the subcontractors essentially did whatever was asked of them. Which is why whenever he gets on the phone with a contractor, they'll 100% price the works for him, show up to site when required, and so on. This is a great example of management. On the other hand, I've experienced managers who micro-manage, burn relationships, and have no self-awareness in the workplace with zero intention to improve on themselves either. It goes without saying one is more conducive to success than others. You create your own management style from the macro to the micro and considering how many years of management will be associated with your career, you cannot leave this to chance. You cannot move through your career with a lack of consciousness about how you are managing people.

Having a one style fits all approach is insufficient in the workplace today, where everyone has alternative intrinsic motivators, and requires different types of management styles. This is why I mentioned the story of the site manager who can read people quickly. Micro-managing someone who needs to work independently and is focused on results won't bring out the best in them. If anything, your best employees may end up leaving. Don't let your lack of honest, authentic, malleable management style become your undoing or your roadblock.

So, how do you figure out your own management style? Consider the following in the development of it:

- Reflect on the positives and negatives of your past management experiences from others and how certain situations made you feel—invigorated or frustrated?
- Ask for feedback from subordinates about your management and be open to receiving honest feedback without getting on the defensive.

- Reflect on what comes naturally to you. For me, being direct and straight to the point comes naturally. You won't see me being casual in giving direction or beating around the bush. Having awareness of this will help tailor your own style.

- Develop and exercise emotional intelligence to learn how to tailor and pivot your style. Being a clinical manager will stifle your opportunities and ability to get people on board.

- Consider the experience you would like your team to have when working with you. Develop your style with your team and colleagues in mind that will benefit yourself, the team, and the business.

There will be situations and scenarios within your workplace that will require you to not only manage downstream but also managing up. Managing up is managing your manager. I'd a mentee of mine who worked on a huge project, coming from a tier 3 background. While he'd technically one manager to report to directly, there was a secondary manager who also demanded tasks and added responsibility to him. This created a conflict in the priorities handed to him at work, and on large projects, one task can take days because of the sheer volume involved. He would work on one task, only to be in a continuous cycle of not meeting the expectations of the other manager. In this scenario, he needed to manage up and manage his time, their time and expectations to maintain the priorities and output.

It's also the consequence when managers themselves are swamped, unorganised, and generally poor at managing themselves that you may find you may be on the receiving end of all this. It can look like being handed a task the night before its due, being set unrealistic deadlines, or not getting the clarity of information you need to proceed with your work. Said inadequate managers can then deem it a reflection of you if you don't rise to challenge or meet their unrealistic expectations. This is when, again, you need to manage up.

This is predominant in construction where there is a myriad of daily demands set down by the client who may not always know what's involved in delivering a response. A manager can move this up your priority chain, but you already have several other priorities.

You may face this situation of being the recipient of conflicting priorities and expectations, and you can't expect management to see this as an issue. There are more than enough managers who have a silo view of what needs to get done and when. This is when you have to manage up. You're communicating and managing the expectations back to them, in the ambition of making their job easier, which makes yours more palatable too. You need to have input into how you are managed, because if this is also left to chance, you may find yourself having a stressful experience or hating what you do.

The first step to managing up is to open up the communication channels with all parties and getting their buy-in and acknowledgement of what the current priorities are. This way, everyone is in concurrence with what will get done and by when. Getting buy-in early on is important. It also demonstrates you are taking authority and ownership about what needs to get done by having a plan. To demonstrate even more initiative, plan ahead with your relevant managers what you will work on as it shows you are anticipating the works that's required, and are working toward meeting deadlines. You can't over-communicate when you're managing up, so increase it.

Second, managing up is also about setting parameters around expectations. Your manager may assume a task takes two hours, but if you don't have the same level of experience, it may take you four. Make that clear from the outset, including the assistance and resources you'll require to get the task done. If your manager is ineffective at managing their own time and sending you tasks at 9pm to be completed by 8am tomorrow, that just won't work. When you manage up, you set the expectation as to the notice period for being assigned tasks and how long it will take you. (Not in consideration of a 10- or 15-minute task which can easily be completed.)

Managing up is also knowing how you work, or like to work, and then clearly relaying that to your manager. Don't assume they know how your day is structured, or what your natural talents are. Openly tell your manager how you like working, how you like being communicated with, and so on. I operate fast, so for me it's a nightmare to mull over one point for forty minutes, when it could have been a five-minute conversation. Explain up the stream your management preferences, because after all, it will benefit everyone involved.

And finally, when managing up, make sure you deliver on the set priorities and expectations. You've now taken the onus of managing them and committing to when it will get done, so it has to be delivered. Don't just talk the talk, have fancy spreadsheets and plans; deliver on it. Not only does this reflect excellently on you but creates reprieve for your manager knowing the work is getting done.

Utilising this behaviour will not only demonstrate your management ability but will enable you to learn the intricacies of management a lot quicker. Isn't it easier to say you're ready for that promotion as you've already been managing the team?

There are still managers in the industry which are considered as old school. They learned their behaviour, operation and management styles from an outdated management system. So, what you get in the workplace is senior managers who can be hard on their teams. My advice to you on this is, don't be disillusioned with the hard ones. Take the good from them, because they have a wealth of industry experience, and leave the bad. They're operating out of a framework where they know what's good from a technical and professional practice standpoint. What you need to look for is who has in the past worked under these 'tough' managers, and where are they now. It is the toughest experiences which shape you, after all.

Leadership

"The greatest leader is not necessarily the one who does the greatest things. He is the one that gets the people to do the greatest things."
Ronald Reagan

In attaining higher compensation, faster progression and more career recognition, there is one all-encompassing requirement you need to fulfil; and that is leadership. This is where you surpass the management level and take your career to new heights.

Leadership in the contemporary workplace looks different from the textbook leadership that is employed. Sentiments are changing in the workplace as younger generations are coming through, who place far more importance on attaining and attaching meaning to their work than just being 'a number' in an organisation. Organisations today have pressures to accommodate for meeting the new expectations of the generation coming through. They don't value autocratic ways and old school ways of doing things. They don't only want to know what to do, but why they are doing it. And they're more concerned with flexibility, personal contribution, being valued, and having meaning in the work (meaningful work that was previously discussed). This is important to understand because if you approach leadership from an expectation that external motivators will suffice, you'll be surprised. Tapping into the intrinsic motivators of the people in your workplace is the new norm. Staying abreast of the current workplace construction and what professionals are seeking from the workplace is an important first step towards constructing your leadership mindset.

Let's get clear again that management does not mean leadership. American educator, author, businessman and keynote speaker Stephen Covey notes, "Management is efficiency in climbing the ladder of success; leadership determines whether the ladder is leaning against the right wall." Leadership is about determining trajectory. Managing others is about making sure others do a task in accordance with the parameters, resources and tools at hand. Management is fundamentally centred on control; which leadership is not. Let's not be mistaken, it requires great management. Without managers, systems and processes fall apart. We need managers to plan, measure, monitor, coordinate, decide, hire, fire, and so many other business functions. But that doesn't mean that they lead people. Leaders lead people.

There is ample discourse and literature around leadership, and it has to be one of the most loosely applied terms in contemporary language. Leadership isn't a title that is attained, it's a way of life, and it permeates everything that you do. Leading authority on leadership

John Maxwell defines leadership as: "… influence - nothing more, nothing less." American business magnate, software developer, investor and philanthropist Bill Gates correctly says that, "Leaders will be those who empower others."

Agreeably, not everyone should be a leader, because there are some who take advantage of such a title and do nothing good with it. It isn't an attribute reserved for the upper echelon of an organisation. Leadership has nothing to do with titles or positions and is not developed in a onetime seminar that focuses heavily on skill acquisition.

I fundamentally understand leadership to be this: a leader has a strong vision, and reasons why. They're able to tie that vision and 'why', with the vision and 'why' of their followers, allowing them to lead people in a direction. The why of the leader and the why of the individual are so intrinsically matched that the follower must follow. A leader is not a leader if no one is following. That's a key marker of a leader—are people willingly and actively going where you wish to go? Leadership is also fundamentally about ensuring other people achieve their own version of success. The success of others is of equal and greater importance than your own, for if others succeed under your leadership, then you have too.

That's why the internal work and management of self has to happen first before you can become a leader. It's not automatic, you need to build up to it. Inherently, everything you've been learning from page 1 is establishing your capacity for leadership, from knowing your why through to networking and now through to understanding leadership.

There are fundamental leadership questions which you can ask yourself. I frequently re-ask myself these questions, as leadership is a continuous process, and requires lots of reorientation and navigation. Because I'm fundamentally dealing with people and that is the greatest variable within itself. Leadership is a process of continuous innovation and maturity, and sometimes you don't know how effective of a leader you have been until you get the feedback loop from people you've positively impacted. It's a lifelong endeavour of which you constantly have to be a student. Consider the following questions about yourself as you discover and constructing your leadership proposition and value:

- Do I raise people up and bring people along with me?
- Am I inspiring and motivating?
- Do I care about the success of others as I do my own?
- Have I reached a level of self-mastery and management?
- Can I build effective and lasting relationships?
- Do I have influential communication ability?
- Can I give constructive and objective feedback?
- Can I delegate with ease?
- Do I have control over my time and priorities?
- Am I able to make decisions and back the decisions of my team?
- Am I able to coach and mentor others?

As I mentioned before, you must have a deep understanding of yourself, and management of your own self before you are capable to lead others and have a leader's mindset. A leader's mindset is acquired and constructed through a commitment to ongoing learning, listening, mentoring, coaching, experience, mistakes and innovative thinking.

> *"Leadership is lifting a person's vision to high sights,*
> *the raising of a person's performance to a higher*
> *standard, the building of a personality beyond its*
> *normal limitations."*
> **Peter Drucker**

Modelling behaviour of exceptional leaders is a great way to learn and apply from successful leaders you admire. Take John Maxwell, for example. There is ample literature about his leadership philosophy you can dissect and understand what makes *them* successful? Why are they considered influential leaders? For me, the first leadership philosophy I integrated into my own was Richard Branson. What drew me in is that he is the only entrepreneur who has built eight separate billion-dollar companies in different industries; so he must have something to say on leadership. It's valuable you study the past and present leaders so you can be a future leader. If you look to your immediate arena, there may not be exceptional examples of leaders, so you need to look much further and outwards.Sometimes seeing poor examples of leadership is useful to outline what makes for a successful leader, because it's obvious what they should be doing. While the core components of a leader is a book within itself, consider the following as you develop your leadership attributes:

1. A leader is to be inspiring and motivating at the least, for that's the basic emotion you can elicit in someone else.
2. A leader looks to the future for solutions instead of relying on existing or past models to solve problems—they're innovative.

3. A leader maintains a high level of integrity by doing what they say and not expecting others to do something they wouldn't do.
4. A leader has exceptional communication ability which is demonstrated via listening and speaking.
5. A leader has a vision for the future and can influence and impact others to translate that to reality while bringing others along.

Not everyone also wants to be a leader. There is just as much opportunity for oneself by being a loyal follower. But to rise to a level in your career that allows you to construct others along with yourself is worth pursuing.

MAINTENANCE

"Keep on going, and the chances are that you will stumble on something, perhaps when you are least expecting it. I've never heard of anyone ever stumbling on something sitting down."
Charles F. Kettering

How fantastic would it all be if you could control every single variable in your career and just have the smoothest run possible? I hope you didn't say that would be great because that's one bland reality. Imagine having vanilla ice-cream for the rest of your life. Your career will present many challenges that will constantly look different at every stage you're at. Like servicing a building, you must apply a level of maintenance to your career. Just like a building has a dedicated facilities management team, so does your career. Except that team is just you.

It's not just your bank balance, body and car that need frequent servicing and maintenance. Your career needs it too. On the back of my podcast launch, I'd a project coordinator in industry message me to say how he was setting aside time each week now to listen to the podcast and check-in on his career. Weekly! Some people don't do it monthly, or once a decade. An easy way to do a check-up is to:

- Track progress against your goals set for the period.
- Take stock of all the career-related achievements (inside and outside of work). If you can't stop writing, well done! If you're scratching around for ideas, it is clear something needs to change: you. Either you're not putting in sufficient effort to yield results, or the organisation is not aligned with your goals to allow for this.
- List a minimum of five reasons you are working at your current workplace. If you list reasons such as great projects, great people, kicking goals, you're on track. If your reasons are you're waiting for long-service benefits, it's time to rethink your workplace.
- Reflect on your plan and goals as set earlier which are a baseline against where you are right now.

This is imperative to make sure you're not just going through the motions in your career, which has just turned into a job you're living for the weekend for. Ask yourself, why are you settling for anything less than excellent? Why are you choosing to stay at a workplace that clearly isn't right for you? I've spoken about it intermittently throughout the book, but now I'll focus on a question we'll all be, or have been challenged by in our careers: should I stay or should

I go? There is a lot of emotion, underlying assumptions and fear around considering leaving a company in pursuit of better sites. For some, there're no sentimentalities, it's just business. However, in the years of mentoring I've been providing, the most emotionally rife conversations are ones around transitioning. I remember the first time I needed to hand in notice and transition. This is another thing no one prepares you for. I was extremely nerve-wracked and worried as to their feedback and response, yet also cementing the reality I was leaving the known and familiar into the unknown. As an once junior in the industry, it was all new. You go through the elated process of interviewing, getting an offer and signing it in excitement, only to then realise the not-so pleasant part of the move has to be made. The second time I moved was a lot easier, because I knew what to anticipate and I'd experience with vetting companies and was much more determined and future focused. I was told I was making a big mistake, and in not so many words, throwing away my future. Well, how wrong that was then, as it is now. You'll also find fear-mongering a tactic from non-exceptional "leaders" to make you debase your decision. When you're looking to leave, make sure that decision is cemented. The game of playing one offer against your existing employer to attain more benefits will hinder you dramatically. Maybe you received what you wanted in the short term (pay), but you've debased your integrity and character. The people you work with will highly likely always think you're playing the market, sitting on the fence and ready to go. If you've decided to leave, be resolute about it and go. The construction industry is notoriously small, so when you are heading out the door, leave as you came in, with appreciation and integrity. Because people move around, you can be working with the same people again. And if you've burned your bridges, you've done your future prospects no favours.

Whenever I get a mentoring client wanting to leave, the first question I ask is why. If it's as simple as an opportunity that you cannot turn down, that is tied to your goals, plan and purpose, then it's a no-brainer at times. On the proviso you've done your due diligence. That's a pull motivation to move, something external is pulling you forward. Other times, it will be a push motivation. Internal factors either within the organisation or within yourself have alerted you it's time to move. If you're staying at an organisation for external trappings of success, you'll stagnate in your career fast. The first and most frequent problem you'll encounter in the workplace will centre on people. In all actuality, this may be the sole reason anyone ever leaves an organisation, it always comes down to people problems first, money second. I may as well just guarantee this. When there are problems in the workplace, the default position is to go into victim mentality and blame others for what is going on. For the situation which is "against you" or things in the workplace are not shaping up as you anticipated, the average professional will be quick to pass the blame onto others. Situations at work can be quickly distorted through feelings. When you lead and navigate based on your feelings, you're hurting your career prospects. The issue with responding to situations based on your emotional state is your emotional state fluctuates and therefore won't ever deliver consistent results. When you feel good, you make good decisions, and vice versa. This is a method of ensuring your level of recognition for the work you do will also fluctuate. To assess a situation at work, you need to provide evidence for all your underlying assumptions and to properly handle a situation, especially when there are people involved. Can someone really argue with indisputable evidence? No, but they can argue with how you feel about a certain situation. This is not dissimilar from the extreme ownership principle which was previously explored. If there is sound evidence a situation at work is not your own doing, and it's highlighted issues are holding your career back, it may be time to move.

The second most pressing factor that will instigate a move is culture. The culture in the workplace may not be the same as from when you started. In construction, site-based teams have cultures within. In cases where the site-culture is not conducive to your wellbeing at work, move sites before you move organisations. Cultures can change quickly when there is a change of management, either in structure or in personnel. If a culture is stifling, backwards, and lacks important values core to you, again, it may be time to go. An organisation may have changed its business plan along the way, undergone a merger acquisition, or has a new strategy. Change is a word that elicits fear within people because they immediately revert to their own situation and fear the job security. Some don't wait to ride out the change and jump before the ship sinks. In other cases, the new organisation doesn't align with the vision and goals anymore, so again, it may be time to go. Then there are the less obvious reasons we may require a move. When you're not being developed and challenged at work can have huge adverse effects. For people who are highly ambitious and move fast, having work that offers no mental stimulation is a nightmare. If the nature of your job is fixed and there are no internal opportunities, you may require a move to stimulate your career again. If there is an evident situation where there is little to no opportunity for growth and development, and no advancement opportunities, it's time to go.

To circle back to where we started, people move because of people. A lack of autonomy or trust may be prevalent, along with not being appreciated or recognised. It won't be the first or last time bad management will push people out. When this happens, the feeling of being stressed out because of the people you work with will have a toll. I hate seeing situations like this when people think they have no choice and to put up with it. There is always a choice.

If your reasons for leaving an organisation are made in the greater good of your future, your vision and your goals, then make the move. Sitting on the fence speculating won't yield results. You don't necessarily have to find a forever company, but one aligned to where you are going right now. And if such a company doesn't exist, remember, you can always build it yourself.

Transitioning

"We keep on moving forward, opening new doors,
and doing new things because we're curious and
curiosity keeps leading us down new paths."
Walt Disney

I've spoken about it intermittently throughout the book about transitioning within your career, but now I'll go into a deeper discussion around this. Transitioning either into construction or from a different sector often has little to do with the individual, but the limited perception by others. Remember, I said before you are not your job title. Except job titles are there to make it easier and more convenient for others to map out a linear career path for you and go through a tick-box exercise. "Well, if they worked as a project manager then they'll be fine as a… marketing manager?" A stretch of an example, but you have the ambition, the passion, transferable skills and experiences, yet transition even between sectors has not been made easy by others. What adds to the exacerbation is that there is an expectation if you transition, you're meant to start at the bottom again. This can seem daunting, especially if you are well advanced into your career. So, what will you do about it?

The first thing is to remember your career is a business which offers a unique value proposition. And as a business, you are required to sell. It is your responsibility to relay your suitability, potential and extreme capability to fulfil the role you are seeking to transition into, regardless of how diverse it is from your background. You are the one who needs to convince and promote yourself, because in these situations, hiring managers and recruiters are not always the ones best positioned to do so. Companies want to find the circular peg to fit in the circular hole when fulfilling a position or creating a new opportunity, because it's the path of least resistance. That doesn't mean it's the path which will yield the greatest results by attracting the highest talent available.

You need to first identify the reasons for the transition and be able to articulate them well. This personal story is what will obtain your initial buy-in and interest from others. The second is to appropriately frame your experiences. When I am mentoring graduates to get into the industry, I always tell them this. It is their responsibility to make sure the reader of their CV has no avoidance of doubt what they are capable of and who they are. The same goes for transitioning. Highlight aspects of your experiences which are most applicable to the sector or industry you are looking to get into. Leadership is universal for example; project management principles are too. The most transferable attributes and skills really need to be exemplified under the umbrella of how this will benefit your future role.

In construction, there is also a tendency to be locked into a certain project typology. If you've forever worked on apartments, transitioning into educational work as an example, will present a challenge. What you need to highlight is the specific knowledge set of apartments applicable to educational builds. This could draw parallels between the similarities in structure and finishing trades you already know. Focus on what you know and amplify that, rather than the gaps. If you've forever worked in fit-out and finally want to venture into new build, look at what aspects are most applicable. It could be intense knowledge of services and high-end finishes. There are many project managers who have been internally promoted within organisations who do not have full exposure and experience with all trades. What they have is the process framework and ability to learn and understand from the people around them.

Your network and ability to develop yourself are even more important when you're looking to transition. Your network will provide you with people who can vouch for your results and capabilities and also provide you with the references and off-market opportunities you need. Also required is your ability to develop yourself, because there are avenues in which you can upskill to demonstrate further capability.

What I find is transitioning often has less to do with one's concern about a potential pay decrease but more about an increasing and constantly resurfacing level of self-doubt. When one looks to transition, the first thing they do is a stock-take of their strengths, which I've discussed. They can easily see the application, the wealth of their experiences and beyond all doubt they can fulfil a role that has nothing to do with the sector or industry they've been in. Yet as soon as you're hitting the market, it's full of friction and resistance. It's filled with people telling you you're not capable enough, not experienced enough, not skilled enough. Just not enough. Hearing that time and time again from people considered knowledgeable about the industry can wear someone down. It can make them question themselves and lose a lot of self-confidence and lose sight. What's happening is other people projecting their own limitations and limited beliefs onto someone else. How original! But by now you will appreciate you have all it takes to construct your career, and the importance of persistence. One of my favourite quotes is "Success is 99% failure" by Soichiro Honda, founder of Honda Motor Co. You only need one yes, one opportunity to transition, and that's exactly what you'll get with the right approach and mindset which I've just discussed.

Mindset

"In the growth mindset, it's almost inconceivable to want something badly, to think you have a chance to achieve it, and then do nothing about it."
Carol Dweck

Throughout this book, explicitly or inadvertently, I've been sharing insights and tactical tools to work on your mindset. I'm sure there are concepts you firmly don't agree with, and concepts that have given you food for thought. Either way, I'm glad, because you're therefore thinking. Your mindset is the most important asset you must continually maintain and develop. This doesn't stop. In her book, 'Mindset: The New Psychology of Success', Dr. Carol S. Dweck identifies two basic mindsets that shape our lives: the fixed mindset and the growth mindset. Fixed mindsets are just that—locked in, unwilling to change, and assumes our character, intelligence and creative ability are static. The growth mindset, on the other hand, is an understanding we can develop all the above. Your mindset can change and is centred on a passion for continuous learning instead of hunger for approval. As Dweck writes; "The passion for stretching yourself and sticking to it, even (or especially) when it's not going well, is the hallmark of the growth mindset. This is the mindset that allows people to thrive during some of the most challenging times in their lives."

When I upgraded my mindset, I changed my life. It is that transformative of an experience, that by not actively doing so, is doing an injustice to your existence. Constantly constructing your mindset is not just about your career, it's about your entire consciousness and life. The consequence of not upgrading your mindset is having a wasted potential, missing opportunities and limiting what is possible. I am certain none of you reading this, want that. Here are ten simple ways which you can immediately employ to get into a growth mindset:

1. Pay attention to your thoughts and words and replace the negative with the positive. Start censoring limiting beliefs that come into mind immediately.
2. Start collecting experiences by pushing yourself into new formative situations.
3. Take pride and joy in the journey and the process, not just the end result.
4. Focus on learning, not failing, as you either win or you learn.
5. Stop seeking approval, as consensus should never trump learning.

6. Accept challenges are part of the journey and as disguised opportunities.
7. Place extra value on consistent effort on the path to mastery.
8. Find lessons and inspiration from the success of others.
9. Surround yourself with growth minded people.
10. Be grateful for criticism and be open to hearing suggestions.

A growth mindset is inherently a positive mindset too. Throughout your career, as I've discussed, you will face challenges that will look different each time. There is intense power in positive thinking, but positive thinking yields positive results. This is not always immediate, or 'not yet'. A positive mindset is a habit and a choice, and a permanent framework in which you can view everything. Because of the longevity of your career, or the extent of trials and tribulations that will come your way, a positive mindset is an essential tool in your toolkit.

CONCLUSION

I wrote this book from a place to guide, inspire and direct you to achieve more recognition, higher compensation and faster career progression. I have shared insights I gathered over the course of my career; insights I have deeply considered shaped my own career. I have parted insights with you I had, or I wish I had as I was propelling through my own career. That's because I know what it's like to feel lost, stuck, stagnated and wanting to turn to just one resource to tell me what I wanted to know. I deeply relate to the feeling of wanting a guide and direction, so it's been my pleasure and privilege to pass this on to you.

Each sentence is a thought that somewhere along my journey has helped get me to where I am today. I realised that unlike live content creation, this book will serve as a snapshot in time of my career intelligence. But for you, I hope it will serve as a lifelong guide and source of inspiration to realise every realm of your potential, and to take extreme ownership over every aspect of your career and life. It's important you stay in your own lane and don't compare your journey to that of others. What I don't want this book to turn into is another self-help resource. The one thing you need to do out of all the things is to take action. Inspiration without action is like turning on the car and going nowhere. The engine is revving, but you're still in park mode and the handbrake is on. The action is where the transformation lies, and is what will transform your career fast, before your eyes. A key part of taking action is persistence. You will only improve via applying, assessing and improving. But you can't improve if there is no action in the first place. Wherever you are on your journey in construction, it is never too late and never too early to construct your career. I truly hope you realise how powerful you truly are, and how much ability you have to control your own trajectory. It's all up to you—hoping that instils inspiration and not dread and overwhelm. The greatest awakening is that of your own consciousness and I trust you now know you are the architect and builder of your own career.

I want to see you win. I want to see you achieve exemplary things in your career, and I want to see you attain all the success you desire.

Elinor Moshe

CONSTRUCTION MANAGEMENT GRADUATES

Bonus Section

I know people in a variety of stages within their career will be reading this book. That's why I wanted to maintain the structure of the book to be as openly applicable to anyone constructing their career. I also know there are people who are looking to get their first job within the industry who will also pick up this book. One of my programs and events is Fast Foundations, which is a holistic service for students and graduates to fast-track career planning, development and also how to attain employment. I teach them how to position themselves in a diluted market to stand out, which is even more important. I've loved receiving the messages of success when those who have worked with me have applied, persisted, and finally got their foot through the door. I know it makes this even more difficult for international students, where they have an additional layer of challenges atop a competitive market.

So, this bonus section is for the graduates looking to secure your first industry position. I'll include bonus content on CV writing and interviewing, and also a consolidated guide to not just what the entry-level roles in construction are, but also what they entail. It's common for graduates to not know what entry-level positions entail. Project coordinator means little until you're working as one. So, if you're a graduate, listen up! I'm talking to you now. The first part of attaining employment is to employ everything I have already written about in this book. I could cut it here now but let me explain it to you. To attract opportunity, you must stand out. And that's done, on an elementary plane, by articulating your passion, your core attributes and your value to the industry. Yes, even as a graduate, you have value to give. It's never been more important to stand out in a market that constantly has a fresh supply of graduates. And it's a common frustration in this market, that you feel invisible after you graduate. Those who undertake Fast Foundations with me aren't invisible in the industry anymore. You get seen. But let's go deeper into this. The first thing you need to shake off is to stop seeing yourself as a "construction management student" but as a "construction management professional". You can't rely on your degree for much anymore. Definitely not to stand out; because all graduates entering the market have a degree which is a common good. If you're going into the market on the sole premise you have a degree and would like employment, I can assure you that it won't happen when you'd like it to happen. The academic system has falsely promised you if you attain a degree and all the necessary learning, you'll get a job. And that's where the shock to your system occurs when you find out it doesn't quite happen that way. In Australia, marks also nearly don't matter, and when they do, they carry little weight. This is contrary to overseas markets, where top grades get you top jobs. If the first sentence on your CV is "I am a construction management student seeking employment…" you have just about culled your chances of ever getting in the interview room.

Second, is to seek employment as soon as possible. I frequently get asked if students should wait until they graduate to attain employment. The short answer is absolutely not. The long answer is this: if you're only starting to seek employment after you graduate, it's you and thousands of other candidates flooding the market at once. Once you graduate, it could take six months, a year—an indefinite period to attain employment, whereas your intention was to probably already be working once you've graduated. This all stems from the underlying philosophy a degree is required to begin your career in construction, but if you've read the whole book, you'll see that it's not. You need to prime yourself for employment from day one. You need to get ready so when an opportunity presents itself, you're ready. That takes time within itself, so you need to start well in advance of when you want to attain employment. When I graduated from my architecture degree, I'd done zero work to prepare myself for attaining employment. Zero, I kid you not! Then a professor at university recommended me for an interview. I hadn't spent semester preparing my folio, so I only went in with my last semester design posters. I didn't have a CV, and I'd no ability to interview. It's obvious to say what the outcome of that interview was. In retrospect, it was meant to happen that way. I left the interview room, with my posters and falling apart model in hand, and made this promise to myself: I will always be ready for an opportunity. I will never let my lack of preparation be the cause of my lack of success.

As a graduate, you need to remember you have an automatic network. It's the peers and staff at university. Your peers will be working in industry and can be your 'in'. The academic staff at universities are well-connected to industry, and organisations do frequently ask them for their top picks. Who do you think your construction professor will recommend? The student who comes late to every class and is on the phone the whole time? Or the student who is actively engaged in class and presents a level of effort on assignments and makes an effort to talk to the lecturers and tutors? The latter, of course. If you have already made the commitment to be at university, milk it! Make use of the time you are there and the investment.

Third, is to realise this process means you'll face many rejections, a lot of no responses, and much discomfort. Get used to it. When I graduated from my architecture degree (and after that fateful interview), I went down the conventional path of emailing my CV with a generic opener and email in ambition to attract leads. I sent over fifty, and I got one kind "no thank you" and one noting my CV was great but they're not hiring. The rejection piece is probably the hardest piece graduates face, because I know you go into an interview wanting a certain outcome. So, you can finally get your foot through the door, earn money, and stop having to go through the process. But it is rife with rejection, and you must move on from it. A no is just getting you closer and closer to the one yes you need. A no just means you got interviewing experience, you got to present yourself. The aftermath of a no is inconsequential. The aftermath of a yes has infinite opportunity, potential and achievement. That's where your focus will be. There are many reasons for not securing a position, but only focus on the ones you can control. There's little to do if they hired someone else based on a better cultural fit or they possessed experience.

Which leads me to my next point. A common misconception graduates face is you can't get a position without experience. I have to remind you—everyone started off in something with no experience. Do you think a CEO was born as a CEO? Do you think the person who has even been working for one year had any experience before that? Probably not. We ALL start off with no experience. It doesn't help that certain agencies and companies advertise for entry-level positions with three years' experience. That's not an entry-level position. The experience factor is not a qualifier or a barrier; it is a false story you're telling yourself that's holding you back.

Maintaining your eye on the prize will be your biggest challenge but realise where you are right now (unemployed) is not a projection of your entire future. That's why I always start off Fast Foundations with the planning aspect. Time and time again, graduates get positions; they get their foot through the door. If they can do it, you can do it. When you see people get positions, you don't see the months and months of consistent work and effort that goes into it. They're just the ones who didn't give up. I'd a mentoring client who wanted to work in infrastructure consultancy and came to me for mentoring because she was at the end of the line. She'd spent months and months networking, volunteering, studying, going for coffees. By the book, she'd done everything required. My advice was simple, keep going. She'd a coffee catch up scheduled with a quantity surveying firm that work on major infrastructure projects. Fast forward, she got the position. Had she given up too soon, that wouldn't have happened. If you're looking for your next position, I'm sorry, but you don't have the luxury of giving up, or even considering it.

Other than the tactical pieces such as having a standout CV and knowing how to interview to convert the opportunity, there are two aspects which graduates fail on developing to fast-track the process: networking and volunteering. I have discussed networking in depth and the advice is relevant and applicable all the same. Once a job is posted online, it's too late. Submitting your CV to mass online recruitment platforms is a void activity. It's an algorithm, not a human reviewing your CV, and the chances of it getting to a human are low. Let alone one who will see you as fitting and will call you. I don't know anyone who has successfully attained a position this way and I know many people. So, I won't rehash the networking advice, but I will address the most common barriers graduates have with networking:

- Yes, you are interesting enough to network, and it's not all about you. Networking is a value exchange, and I am sure you can go to an event and be interested in others. If you don't consider yourself interesting, then go back to page 1 and do the work.
- Networking can come naturally to some, but it is also a learned skill. You can learn how to network just like you can learn to ride a bike. Saying you don't know how to network is just an excuse that can be overcome. The real concern is….
- Confidence. This is a concern for people at any level throughout. Confidence comes AFTER you take action on what scares you the most. (Networking is not the scariest thing, I promise.) Confidence comes once you put yourself in networking situations again and again and realise it's just being in a room talking to people. Are you concerned you'll say something "wrong"? People won't remember it in five minutes, let alone five months.

But I will elaborate on the volunteering piece. Even if you don't have part-time work experience (retail or hospitality are common) then volunteering is the easiest avenue to gain "experience". When you volunteer, it shows you're motivated enough to dedicate yourself to something else and contribute to a community. I've spoken about the importance of aligning yourself with an industry association. Volunteering allows to you have access to key attribute development the construction industry looks for when hiring: initiative, communication, ability to work in a team, be self-motivated, driven, and so on. If you've organised industry events as part of a university association for example, you're developing your organisational, time management and planning skills, while able to coordinate with external stakeholders. This is not too dissimilar to what you'll be doing on the job. There are ample opportunities to volunteer, and it's an easy way to get professional connections and valid experience. This is an easy way to stand out. Think about it. Who are the students you remember from your cohort? They're the active ones, part of the associations and events held. Who do you think industry notices best?

Companies are also not hiring you as a graduate with no professional experience on your extreme technical aptitude. They're not hiring you on your ability to "Make $20M in revenue in the first year!" And graduates typically approach the marketplace on the sales point of their technical ability. You're not an expert in negotiation and management—a bit of an overstretch at this stage. What you need to highlight and show are your values, your passion, your attributes. Companies want to see your long-term vision, your ability to learn and grow, your drive and dedication. This is what will make them want to give you a chance. They can teach you all the technical skills, but they can't teach you work-ethic and drive.

There's one final aspect of job seeking which I need to quell. And it's being lazy about it. Sending someone your CV on LinkedIn and expecting them to find a job for you won't work. Why should anyone do your work for you, if you're not even able to learn how to do it? Another is to simply approach people, whether it is online or offline, and immediately ask for a position. No one owes you anything. As harsh as it sounds, that's how it is. You must demonstrate why someone should have a conversation with you. Why someone should look at your CV. Laziness is also approaching the job hunt via one medium. It's far more involved than that. Sitting behind a computer sending out CVs won't get you the results you want. You need to approach job hunting like a full-time job.

The things I've spoken about, such as LinkedIn, mentoring and the like, are just as applicable to job seeking as it is propelling your career. The same about being specific in your search. Graduates tend to go wide instead of deep. We all know now you'll miss 100% of the targets you didn't set. If you're not aiming for a particular position in a particular sector, you'll miss a lot of shots. This is contrary advice to advice to just apply, apply, apply. How's that working out for you? Not great. Because you need to focus your efforts and resources.

Now, a CV is one way to get yourself in front of prospective employers. Quite frankly, with the rise of video and so many other media channels, I won't be surprised if the CV becomes redundant. In other progressive industries such as technology and digital media, it most has. But in the interim, your CV has one goal—be attractive enough to be read to consider getting you into an interview room. That's the sole point of it. It needs to be a precise package representing who you are, what your value is and a succinct summary of your experiences and skills.

When you're putting your CV together, think about it from the perspective of the person reading it. They're possibly looking at hundreds of CVs, if you're applying to a graduate program, or they're looking for a standout candidate. The same with recruiters—they see a lot of CVs. You have to think, what can I do to make this a standout document that they have *no choice* but to call you in for an interview?

Here are the top 11 considerations when putting together your CV.

- Your CV cannot be any longer than two pages. You need to plan before you execute and look at what is impressive enough and worth mentioning.
- Your CV needs to be designed. A CV doesn't have to be a boring old black and white template with Times New Roman font that looks like an essay. The first thing someone sees when they open it is a visual element—the design, the layout, the colour. Make it look like you spent so much effort putting it together. You don't need to know how to use publisher or InDesign, you can use Microsoft Word templates, and if you're extra dedicated, check out the whole suite of Canva templates. Make it look like a document someone wants to read because it shows the effort you put into it. No bold bright colours, just professional, neutral colours and consistent fonts.
- Have a short, concise paragraph about your career objective to start your CV. This is to demonstrate why you desire to be in the industry and that you have long-term objectives. Your career objective

should clearly articulate your passions, interest and relevant experience (if any). This section is your elevator pitch, and an opportunity to showcase a bit about who you are professionally and personally. It can include your career focus, which highlights what you can do now, outline your core strengths, and how you plan to project that into the future.

- Categorise your CV – I use career objective, work experience, education, professional achievements (which you would switch out for extra-curricular activity), industry participation, and references. You list your current/previous experience in chronological order with the most recent at the top for each section. If you had a part-time job over seven years ago, think about how relevant it is. You can also put your education first if you don't have work experience. If you're relaying international experience, don't assume the local market understands the company size or the work you did. Make sure the references match the local context and it's clear to ascertain the work you've done internationally.

- When talking about your work experience, relevant to industry or not, another common mistake I see is people relaying the job description. i.e. "had to close the store". What this doesn't tell the reader is what you learned and achieved while being in this position. You need to be as specific as possible what you did in your role, and focus on the results, achievements, and skills you attained during your tenure. These help to demonstrate why you will be suitable to interview for this position. It's also valuable to explain how you developed said skill. "I have great capability to work in a team to deliver on outcomes, as during my position I was given the role of team leader". Or "I have excellent client focus as I was responsible for resolving all customer complaints". Or "I have great organisational skills as I was the lead organiser for XYZ event". Demonstrate the key skills and competencies instead of listing them. Just make sure your sentences are short and concise but don't be vague. Get to the point quick.

- It's important to include the project name, size, and value (in AUD) you have worked on. This applies especially if you are translating overseas experience into the local market. There is a difference between working on large infrastructure projects and a house. To paint a fuller picture of your experience; this is a must. Be as specific as possible with the project information without compromising any commercially sensitive information.

- This leads me to say while many entry-level positions are similar, make sure your CV is responsive to the position being advertised and the skills you are highlighting apply. You can refer to the position description and incorporate key words from it, but don't be repetitive.

- Add personal interests and hobbies as this helps to convey character and personality and can also give more insight into who you are. If you love photography and sports, mention it. The same goes if you have volunteered anywhere; describe your volunteering experience in the same weight and regard as a paid position.

- There are two schools of thought on including referencing. In either case, you must have a minimum of two references available, either to include or be available upon request. References can be one academic and one from a previous part-time job, or volunteering role if you haven't worked.

- A common mistake I see when I review CVs is they aren't proofread to check for flow and comprehension. Think, when someone else is reading this, does this build up a holistic picture about who you are, what you're doing, what you're aiming for, and why you're suitable to at least interview. Does it read well?

- Finally, don't lie on your CV. Can you really do this skill you are presenting? Are you 100% competent in this? Don't lie and don't exaggerate. You must be able to back up every point on your CV with an example. If you get found on via being tested in an interview, it won't reflect well on you and your level of honesty and integrity.

The purpose of a CV is to get it out to market when it's at least 90% perfect, because you'll be able to tweak it based on the feedback you're getting. Don't get into an analysis-paralysis mode where you spend all your time working to perfect it but not getting it out there in time. There's no point having a perfect CV if no one sees it. The process itself is iterative, which is why you need the feedback in the first place to get it right.

Cover letters can give you extra space to put your best foot forward and continue to demonstrate how suitable you are to the position. They show how you intend to deliver value to the organisation and showcase why you're the best candidate for the position. I frequently get asked if a cover letter should be submitted and my answer is this; give it all you got the first time round when applying. The person hiring may look for a cover letter first and if you don't have one, you may reduce your chances of your CV being read. Plus, its extra real estate to showcase yourself. Why wouldn't you do it? Remember when you're looking for a job, do everything you can to stand out, and if that means doing a cover letter, then you do it. A cover letter is not a regurgitation of your CV. A cover letter is 3-4 paragraphs further highlighting your alignment and suitability to work with the organisation you are applying for.

1. This can be cumbersome, but for every job you apply for, you need to tailor your cover letter to suit. If you want to demonstrate you're thrilled to be applying for this specific position at this company, it means tailoring the letter to suit. Don't say something like "at your company" because it shows you're probably recycling the letter.

2. Make sure it is made out to the right person. To whom it may concern a no-no, as is "Dear Sir or Madam". The job ad may specify, but if it doesn't, at least go with "Dear Hiring Manager". Make sure you specify the role you are applying for so there is no confusion. Again, if you want to be a cut above

the rest, call the company or recruiter and find out to whom it should be made out.

3. Start your letter with something more than a generic opener. Captivate someone with your passion, what brought you here, maybe something you really admire about the company like their award-winning projects or safety culture. Maybe something humorous if that's your personality or position yourself well again by highlighting a recent achievement or accomplishment. It's OK to be creative.

4. Your cover letter is not a summary of your CV. Don't repeat or regurgitate what's already on there. This is where you can deep dive into a particular experience or event or talk more about a big responsibility or achievement you've had. You can talk about how you align with the company values and culture by doing some research on the company website. Paint a fuller picture of your experiences, accomplishments, your personality, and hone in on *why* you're just perfect for this opportunity. This isn't the space to talk about your education or grades or any of that, and it's another common mistake I see. And it's totally OK to "brag". Now is the time.

5. Keep it to less than a page. This person has a lot to read, so like the CV, make sure it's specific. It has to be professional, but not excessively cold. Let your voice come through and definitely show off some personality.

6. Finish strong. A conventional "I look forward to

hearing from you" is average and not the strongest finish. Your last few lines are your closer as to your enthusiasm, passion for the position, and how you're the best fit. You can say "I'm dedicated to achieving the mission of the company and would bring my excellent drive that is dedicated to achieving project outcomes". Try that next time you're writing.

7. Avoid the overuse of "I". If you start every paragraph with I, mix it up with "My" "This". Anything, really. This isn't all about you. The company has a problem which is a vacancy, and you are providing a solution. Make it about someone else.

8. Ensure this looks like a professional letter in terms of formatting, font, grammar and spacing, and matches the formatting of your CV.

9. Finally, like your CV, proofread again and again. Make sure the content flows, it reads well and answer the questions of – Does this sell me as the best person for the job? Does it get someone thrilled and wanting to know more about me? No spelling errors? Think to yourself, "Would I want to call me in for an interview after reading this?" If you even slightly hesitate about answering yes to any of this, go back and work on it.

As I said, the CV is only the starting point of attaining an opportunity. The magic happens in the interview. This is where the conversion happens. The issue with interviewing is the mindset piece, not the tactical.

I converted zero opportunities in architecture, and in reflection it was for the best, and also because I didn't really have a passion that showed. On the other hand, I have converted every single construction industry interview I have gone for. I bet you want my interviewing insight now. But a lot of that success is premised on doing everything from page 1 first. So, let's break down the behemoth interviews appear to be.

First things first, let's discuss the mindset.

- The stress and anxiety brought on by interviewing is by concentrating on the outcome. Don't focus on the outcome. You can't control the outcome, but you can control the process and everything that goes into it that will help you get the desired outcome. You may have the best interview, walk out of there thinking you got it in the bag, and you get the call you didn't want to hear. Also, you don't know who else has been interviewed, or why they were hired.
- The stress also comes from being underprepared. You can mitigate this by coming prepared. It's the same as an exam. You can fail to prepare and walk into an exam knowing it's a lost cause, fumbling your way through.
- Instead of dreading the interview, flip the conversation and get excited. This is what you have been working towards, so why are you dreading it? That sends out the wrong message to your mind and impacts your ability to attract future opportunities.

- Have resilience. You'll get some no's, or no call backs. You only need one yes, and that may be amongst getting fifty no's. That's totally fine. It hasn't taken away from your grand vision or desires for your career.
- If you're nervous, talk to someone beforehand, get some positive reaffirmation before you go in, or whatever you need. Honestly, you just need to be yourself and present the best version of yourself. Which, by having read my book, you're in a position to do so. Don't be someone or something you're not.

Now, what to do to prepare for the interview:
- If you've gone via a recruiter, find out everything you can about the company—culture, projects, people from them. What are they looking for? What can they tell you about the position? Most importantly, what can they tell you about the person who is interviewing you? Not just professionally, but find out if you can about their interests, you may have something in common.
- If you know someone who works for the company, do the same. Get your insider information. This is why networking has ultra-importance in the early stages of your career.
- Use the company's webpage to get familiar with their values and projects. Especially the key words associated with their values because you want to be using this in the interview, both to demonstrate awareness but also alignment.

- Know your selling points. Why are you a cut above the rest, why should you get this job, what are your reasons? Like your CV, anything you state you're good at has to be backed up with an example. In the actual interview, make it clear what your selling point is, and then back it up with an example. Don't go off on a long story with no start and no end.

- Rehearse with a friend, a mentor, a coach. Rehearse! The internet is full of commonly asked interview questions such as, tell me about yourself, what are you trying to get out of your career, why do you like construction, why should we hire you? Come prepared with mental answers, so you're not shooting blanks in the interview. But please, make sure you rehearse so you can say it in a confident and convincing way. Actors don't start practicing when they're on stage, do they? If you don't want to practice around people, you can also record yourself.

- Plan for your interview day, including how you'll get there, when you need to leave, and what you'll wear.

- Make sure you remember what is on your CV. If it's been awhile between writing it and interviewing, refresh your memory.

Now, what to do on interview day. The part you have been waiting for.

- First, arrive 10-15 minutes before the interview. Don't arrive half an hour early, because that can sometimes stress out the person interviewing you as they know you are early. Despite everything, you must be on time. If you think you're running late because of unforeseen circumstances, call the office and let them know.

- Come prepared – have a copy of your CV, your transcript available in a clean folder. They may or may not look at it, but it shows you have put in consideration and preparation.

- Presentation – I hope this goes without saying but you must wear your Sunday best. Clean attire, smart casual, business shoes. How you present yourself speaks volumes before you do and leans into your personal brand.

- Body language - how many seconds does it take for someone to make a first impression of you? Within the first seven seconds of meeting, people will have a solid impression of who you are. Some research suggests a tenth of a second is all it takes to determine traits like trustworthiness. Body language is part of this. Stand tall, don't slouch, have a firm handshake, look the person in the eye, smile, greet them. Exert confidence, presence, be someone people want to converse with.

- As part of your preparation for the interview, you need to note down questions for the interviewer— intelligent ones, because this shows you're serious about this. If at the end of the interview, they ask you if you have any questions, you must always have some. It shows you are inquisitive and legitimately interested. This will be easy to do after reading this book as we've discussed the company considerations in detail.

- You may ask for insights into the role. What kind of person they are looking for, home in on the career opportunities available, the project you may be working on, who will be on the team, and so on.

- In an interview, never sit there waiting to be asked questions, you are an equal part to this conversation and can use it to sway it to your advantage.

- Before you close, make sure you address any of their concerns. And ensure when you close, you finish on a positive note. I suggest you ask about the timeframe for their decision making as it will indicate when you can expect to hear from them.

- A marker or a good interview is when it's at least one hour. This is in person, and online interviews or over the phone interviews may be shorter as they're looking to shortlist in the first instance.

After all your hard work, the follow up is important. If you have an email, send a note to say thank you, but make it personal by recounting what was discussed. If it was via the recruiter, you can do the same, and make sure if you aren't successful, you seek advice on how you can improve the next time round.

I have saved the best until last. The impassioned discourse on LinkedIn earlier in the book would not be complete without at least ensuring that you're optimizing your LinkedIn page, so when a potential opportunity lands on your page, you're making it worth their while. I tend to think of your LinkedIn page as your home. What do you want people to see and know about you when they come over? Will they see your optimal self, or will they see an incoherent mess strewn all over? The profiles that captivate my attention are those that are personalized, and do not rely on a showcase of technicality and a regurgitation of a job description. The purpose of a profile is to hold attention and facilitate a connection.

Here are the minimum requirements of your LinkedIn profile:

- It has to be complete. There is no excuse for having an incomplete profile. When decision makers and hiring professionals look you up, you cannot afford to have an incomplete profile. This shows inactivity and creates a disconnect between the two parties.

- Include a cover photo, but not one from your last holiday.

- Your profile picture should be clear enough and of suitable proximity so people can see how you look like. Understand that the type of image you put immediately speaks volumes to your personal brand. Plus, pages with photos are 11X more likely to get views. The fundamental premise of being on LinkedIn is to be seen.

- Your tagline is imperative as it is what will get you picked up in searches. There is a huge difference between 'student looking for work' and 'construction management professional'. The more active you are on the platform, the more the algorithm rewards you by appearing in searches. An active user on LinkedIn should appear in 30-

40 searches per day. If you're seeking a project management role, ensure project management is in your tagline.

- The biography part of your LinkedIn profile is prime real estate. This is where your elevator pitch goes, and typically where people go to first when exploring a profile. I personally love reading the passionate, personalized and detailed ones that give a window into who the person is. It's what stands out and makes for a memorable first impression.

- As a graduate, add in any work experience you have had. It shows that you are employable, and potentially have long periods of it with transferrable skills. Of equal weight is inclusion of any volunteering work you have done. Both with your work and voluntary experience, don't just list it. You cannot expect hiring professionals to know what value you derived and how you developed as a result of said position. It's up to you to detail that and not leave it to the assumptions of others.

- The recommendation section is a powerful section of LinkedIn. As a construction management graduate, you already have come across professionals – whether that's volunteering, lecturers, people in your network. Reach out and ask for a recommendation, because they're a valuable form of social currency that are as good as references on your CV.

Optimizations of your LinkedIn profile is not a set and forget activity. It requires constant iteration and review of metrics. Once it is thoroughly complete, ensure that you utilize the platform for its true benefit: bringing in opportunity into your world.

Entry-level positions

Whenever I hold an industry event, the graduates are always keen to speak to someone in industry. With great curiosity of "What do you do?" is frequently asked because understanding how construction management is translated into different roles in the industry is not clear, let alone in a local context. The titles that conventionally cover entry-level positions are mostly as follows:

- Graduate/Junior Estimator
- Building/Project Coordinator
- Assistant Contracts Administrator/Assistant Project Manager
- Site Engineer/Project Engineer
- Cadet/Graduate
- Graduate Quantity Surveyor/Junior Cost Planner
- Assistant Development Manager
- Assistant Building Surveyor
- Assistant Design Manager

This list doesn't include OHS roles, or extensive consultancy roles such as programmers. Site management roles are also available, albeit typically more applicable to those coming through with a trade background and not a management degree. While each position entails different functions, on the whole graduates can fulfil the following functions. This can greatly vary between organisations and management personnel. If it's a contractor side role, you'll be fundamentally involved with and responsible for:

- **Document control** – ensuring only the latest documentation is printed on site and distributed to subcontractors and relevant consultants.
- **Quality assurance** – obtaining and checking quality assurance documents from trades and maintaining relevant internal signoffs.
- **Safety administration** – they may require you to run daily (7am) inductions, ensuring all relevant paperwork is submitted from trades, following up relevant reviews, and keeping relevant registers or platforms up to date.
- **Small package tendering** – you may get to tender small works packages, depending on the size and structure of the project.
- **Meeting minutes** – attending meetings, writing minutes and distributing.
- **Materials order** – this is supporting site management with items required for building construction works and for the site.
- **On-site trade coordination,** including all communication management – you may work under a Contract Administrator who manages a trade package, and you're responsible for the on-site coordination aspect. It again depends on the structure of the team.
- **RFI (Request for Information) and RFA (Request for Approval) management** – you'll be maintaining registers insuring transparency of communication and deadlines.

Assistant Project Management roles that are client-side are not too dissimilar in terms of meeting minutes, document review and control, but have more administrative functions. These may be reviewing basic variations, attending all stakeholder meetings and Project Control Group meetings, reviewing contractor reports, report writing, and maintaining consultant group requirements.

If it's an entry-level estimating position, you'll be fundamentally involved with and responsible for:

- **Calling subcontractors for pricing** – this involves getting on the phone and talking to trades about pricing, including following up to get their submission.
- **Manual take offs** – not everything is priced externally, so you'll be doing manual take offs (with a ruler or a measuring software).
- **Maintaining and updating databases** – this is to know who's pricing works and supporting the estimating department, and entering up-to-date contact details.
- **Vetting quotes** – once the quote comes in, you'll help make sure everything off the drawings has been covered.
- **Assisting tender submissions** – the bid submissions team need a lot of information from the estimating department to get a tender out the door.
- **Document control** – ensuring trades have the latest documentation to price off and include in their submission.

Entry-level quantity surveying roles are not too dissimilar in document control, undertaking take offs, but are more involved in cost planning, cost management and drafting Bill of Quantities.

It is always via networking and conversations with people in industry that you'll gain more insight into the day-to-day of what positions entail as I have discussed previously when trailing out careers.

Your First Day

As I was concluding this bonus section, I realised there is one more aspect which needs to be covered. For many entering industry, it's also the first time you'll be working in a professional environment. It's a big shift from a student lifestyle, dotted with part-time jobs or having no structure to your day whatsoever. Then one day all the searching stops, you sign a contract and start on Monday. The sense of anticipation is unforgettable; it feels like being at the start of something brilliant, part of this inner sanctum. You never forget your first day on the job. Also, because it all comes at you quickly. So, what can you expect when you're starting your first job in construction? (Other than congratulations from everyone.)

- The quantum of hours you must pull will be a temporary shock to the system, which is variable between different types of organisations. Regardless, it will be an increase from your part-time hours. All of a sudden you have to be a functioning, pleasant human at 7am (site-based) or 8am (office-based) and have temperamental finishes. Weekends (if you're not working Saturday if you end up at a tier one firm) will be for sleeping, but you will adjust.

- Speaking of Saturdays, depending on the company you join, working Saturdays may be required, especially if you have a site-based role. If your weekend is important to you, it's obvious you don't join a tier one company in a site-based role.

- You'll feel lost, unsure of what you should be doing, and whether you're doing great. It will feel like everyone has seventy years more experience and has always been so competent. It won't always feel so overwhelming and new, and you'll get assigned more work in due course. Just give yourself time to learn and be.

- Tasks will take you double the time to achieve, because it's new, and that's ok.

- You'll hear so many acronyms and construction-only language. The first acronym I learned was 'RSD'. Roller Shutter Door. Common words such as socks and eyes have a whole different meaning in the construction world. You'll get used to it.

- You'll be asking lots of questions. Ask everyone questions. Yes, there is such a thing as a stupid question, but in the context of learning construction and how it all works, there is none. People will not be critical of you for asking the question. You're better off asking, garnering the knowledge, and learning, rather than sitting there stuck and clueless.

- If you are working for a head contractor, building relationships with subcontractors will be a key to your early success. They're the ones who hold the technical knowledge that you need, not your university degree. Learn as much as you can from all the trades you encounter on site. They are typically more than happy to share their knowledge and expertise with people willing to listen.

But above all, enjoy it. It's the first day of the next chapter of your career. One day you'll look back on it and think how far you've come. That is a truly rewarding feeling.

As graduates, once you enter the industry, there can be a common feeling of, 'Now what do I do?' It's this: never stop working on yourself. Investing in yourself. The learning hasn't ceased with your education, it's only just begun. You're here to work on one project, and that is you.

Want to keep on Constructing Your Career?

Visit elinormoshe.com

ACKNOWLEDGEMENTS

This book would not be complete without taking the chance to say thank you to the people who have been imperative constructing my career and life. The largest and most heartfelt thank you goes to my parents. The level of sacrifice and hard work they have made in their life to ensure we, as a small family unit thrive, is beyond remarkable and commendable. For it is everything they have ever done for me, time and time again, year on year, that has given me every avenue and opportunity to succeed and continue reaching great heights. I'm proud they consider it all worth it when they see my achievements, my success and my happiness, because I attest so much of it to them. To my dad, who I am a next generation copy of, thank you for giving me my blueprint of success, for my headstrong, fearless attitude and for always backing me. To my mum, thank you for doing everything you possibly can for me, and for teaching me to think with my heart and not just my mind.

It also doesn't matter how long you have known someone for, but the impact one person can have on you can change every single facet of your life. To my mentor, Ron Malhotra, thank you for seeing me, for believing in me, for giving me back my power and making sure I never let it go again. There is no other experience in this world akin to working with you. You held up a mirror for me to see clearly and gave me the greatest gifts of all that will forever permeate my mind, heart and soul. Caroline Vass, thank you for believing in my vision and seeing its ever-expansive possibility. You've shown me a version of myself and helped me piece together the puzzle.

I keep a small and tight inner circle, but it's quality over quantity. Thank you to the people in my corner who support everything I do, and not just via words. Via showing up, and cheering, and being consistently there with me. I appreciate you, sitting in the audience of my events, being the first to say congratulations, and to also never let me forget who I am for a second. Thank you to every member of my community. In a world full of distractions and demands, you've chosen to be here. Chosen to have me as your leader, your mentor, your guide, and I do not take that privilege lightly. Thank you for continuing to make the choice to be part of my community. I promise if you continue to come with me, I will take you further and farther than you could have imagined yourself. We're on this ever-expansive journey together, you and I. I know we're not here alone having a human experience. We are mere extensions of the universe. I give my daily thank you and gratitude to the divine presence within us all, for guidance, protection and for giving me the opportunity to be me.

ABOUT THE AUTHOR

Elinor Moshe is an ambitious and driven Thought Leader, founder of *The Construction Coach*, impactful public speaker and panelist, host of industry leading podcast *Constructing You*, and author of *Constructing Your Career*. An experience onto herself, Elinor holds insightful and unforgettable industry events. Her passion in life is to guide, inspire and direct you to work on the greatest project that you ever will - yourself. Ambition and achievement is Elinor's first language, and is a forward-thinking industry leader and dedicated mentor. Elinor lives in Melbourne, Australia.